ADRIENNE RICH

WOMEN OF IDEAS

Series Editor: Liz Stanley
Editorial Board: Cynthia Enloe and Dale Spender

This series consists of short study guides designed to introduce readers to the life, times and work of key women of ideas. The emphasis is very much on the ideas of these women and the political and intellectual circumstances in which their work has been formulated and presented.

The women featured are both contemporary and historical thinkers from a range of disciplines including sociology, economics, psychoanalysis, philosophy, anthropology, history and politics. The series aims to: provide succinct introductions to the ideas of women who have been recognised as major theorists; make the work of major women of ideas accessible to students as well as to the general reader; and appraise and reappraise the work of neglected women of ideas and give them a wider profile.

Each book provides a full bibliography of its subject's writings (where they are easily available) so that readers can continue their study using primary sources.

Books in the series include:

Eleanor Rathbone
Johanna Alberti

Simone de Beauvoir
Mary Evans

Christine Delphy
Stevi Jackson

Adrienne Rich
Liz Yorke

ADRIENNE RICH

Passion, Politics and the Body

Liz Yorke

SAGE Publications
London • Thousand Oaks • New Delhi

Extracts from *Collected Early Poems: 1950–1970* © 1993 by Adrienne Rich. © 1967, 1963, 1962, 1961, 1960, 1959, 1958, 1957, 1956, 1955, 1954, 1953, 1952, 1951 by Adrienne Rich. © 1984, 1975, 1971, 1969, 1966 by W.W. Norton & Company, Inc. Extracts from *The Fact of a Doorframe: Poems Selected and New, 1950–1984* by Adrienne Rich. © 1984 by Adrienne Rich. © 1975, 1978 by W.W. Norton & Company Inc. © 1981 by Adrienne Rich. Extracts from *A Wild Patience Has Taken Me This Far: Poems 1978–1981* by Adrienne Rich. © 1981 by Adrienne Rich. Extracts from *Your Native Land, Your Life: Poems by Adrienne Rich.* © 1986 by Adrienne Rich. Extracts from *Dark Fields of the Republic: Poems 1991–1995* by Adrienne Rich. © 1995 by Adrienne Rich. Extracts from *Time's Power: Poems 1958–1988* by Adrienne Rich. © 1989 by Adrienne Rich. Extracts from *Of Woman Born: Motherhood as Experience and Institution* by Adrienne Rich. © 1986, 1976, by W.W. Norton & Company, Inc. Extracts from *On Lies, Secrets, and Silence: Selected Prose 1966–1978* by Adrienne Rich. © 1979 by W.W. Norton & Company, Inc. Extracts from *Blood, Bread, and Poetry: Selected Prose 1979–1985* by Adrienne Rich. © 1986 by Adrienne Rich. Extracts from *What is Found There: Notebooks on Poetry and Politics* by Adrienne Rich. © 1993 by Adrienne Rich. Reprinted by permission of the author and W.W. Norton & Company, Inc.

First published 1997

SAGE Publications Ltd
6 Bonhill Street
London EC2A 4PU

SAGE Publications Inc
2455 Teller Road
Thousand Oaks, California 91320

SAGE Publications India Pvt Ltd
32, M-Block Market
Greater Kailash – I
New Delhi 110 048

British Library Cataloguing in Publication data

A catalogue record for this book is available
from the British Library.

ISBN 0 8039 7726 3
ISBN 0 8039 7727 1 (pbk)

Library of Congress catalog record available

Typeset by M Rules
Printed in Great Britain by Biddles Ltd, Guildford, Surrey

Contents

For Cynthia, who brings
such joy into my life

Preface

This series introduces readers to the life, times and work of key 'women of ideas' whose work has influenced people and helped change the times in which they lived. Some people might claim that there are few significant women thinkers. However, a litany of the women whose work is discussed in the first titles to be published gives the lie to this: Simone de Beauvoir, Zora Neale Hurston, Simone Weil, Olive Schreiner, Hannah Arendt, Eleanor Rathbone, Christine Delphy, Adrienne Rich, Audre Lorde, to be followed by Rosa Luxemburg, Melanie Klein, Mary Wollstonecraft, Andrea Dworkin and Catherine MacKinnon, Margaret Mead, Charlotte Perkins Gilman, Hélène Cixous, Luce Irigaray and Julia Kristeva, Alexandra Kollontai, and others of a similar stature.

Every reader will want to add their own women of ideas to this list – which proves the point. There *are* major bodies of ideas and theories which women have originated; there *are* significant women thinkers; *but* women's intellectual work, like women's other work, is not taken so seriously nor evaluated so highly as men's. It may be men's perceptions of originality and importance which have shaped the definition and evaluation of women's work, but this does not constitute (nor is there any reason to regard it as) a definitive or universal standard. *Women of Ideas* exists to help change such perceptions, by taking women's past and present production of ideas seriously, and by introducing them to a wide new audience. *Women of Ideas* titles include women whose work is well known from both the past and the present, and also those unfamiliar to modern readers although renowned among their contemporaries. The aim is to make their work accessible by drawing out of what is a frequently diverse and complex body of writing the central ideas and key themes, not least by locating these in relation to the intellectual, political and personal milieux in which this work originated.

Do women of ideas have 'another voice', one distinctive and different from that of men of ideas? or is this an essentialist claim and are ideas at basis unsexed? Certainly women's ideas are differently positioned with regard to their perception and evaluation. It is still a case of women having to be twice as good to be seen as half as good as men, for the apparatus of knowledge/power is configured in ways which do not readily accord women and their work the same status as that of men. However, this does not necessarily mean either that the ideas produced by women are significantly different in kind or, even if they presently are, that this is anything other than the product of the workings of social systems which systematically differentiate between the sexes, with such differences disappearing in an equal and just society. *Women of Ideas* is, among other things, a means of standing back and taking the longer view on such questions, with the series as a whole constituting one of the means of evaluating the 'difference debates', as its authors explore the contributions made by the particular women of ideas that individual titles focus upon.

Popularly, ideas are treated as the product of 'genius', of individual minds inventing what is startlingly original – and absolutely unique to them. However, within feminist thought a different approach is taken, seeing ideas as social products rather than uniquely individual ones, as collective thoughts albeit uttered in the distinctive voices of particular individuals. Here there is a recognition that ideas have a 'historical moment' when they assume their greatest significance – and that 'significance' is neither transhistorical nor transnational, but is, rather, temporally and culturally specific, so that the 'great ideas' of one time and place can seem commonplace or ridiculous in others. Here too the cyclical and social nature of the life of ideas is recognised, in which 'new' ideas may in fact be 'old' ones in up-to-date language and expression. And, perhaps most importantly for the *Women of Ideas* series, there is also a recognition of the frequently *gendered* basis of the judgements of the 'significance' and 'importance' of ideas and bodies of work.

The title of the series is taken from Dale Spender's (1982) *Women of Ideas, and What Men have Done to Them*. 'What men have done to them' is shorthand for a complex process in which bodies of ideas 'vanish', not so much by being deliberately suppressed (although this has happened) as by being trivialised, misrepresented, excluded from the canon of what is deemed good, significant, great. In addition to these gatekeeping processes, there are other broader factors at work. Times change, intellectual fashion changes also. One product of this is the often very different interpretation and understanding of bodies of ideas over time: when looked at from different – unsympathetic – viewpoints, then dramatic shifts in the representation of these can occur. Such shifts in intellectual fashion sometimes occur in their own right, while at other times they are related to wider social, economic and political changes in the world. Wars, the expansion and then contraction of colonialism, revolutions, all have had an effect on what people think, how ideas are interpreted and related to, which ideas are seen as important and which outmoded.

'Women of ideas' of course need not necessarily position themselves as feminists nor prioritise concern with gender. The terms 'feminist' and 'woman' are by no means to be collapsed, but they are not to be treated as binaries either. Some major female thinkers focus on the human condition in order to rethink the nature of reality and thus of 'knowledge'. In doing so they also reposition the nature of ideas. Each of the women featured has produced ideas towards that greater whole which is a more comprehensive rethinking of the nature of knowledge. These women have produced ideas which form bodies of systematic thought, as they have pursued trains of thought over the course of their individual lives. This is not to suggest that such ideas give expression to a 'universal essence' in the way Plato proposed. It is instead to reject rigidly dividing 'realist' from 'idealist' from 'materialist', recognising that aspects of these supposedly categorical distinctions can be brought together to illuminate the extraordinarily complex and fascinating process by which ideas are produced and reproduced in particular intellectual, cultural and historical contexts.

The *Women of Ideas* series is, then, concerned with the 'history of ideas'. It recognises the importance of the 'particular voice' as well as the shared context; it insists on the relevance of the thinker as well as that which is thought. It is concerned with individuals in their relation to wider collectivities and contexts, and it focuses upon the role of particular women of ideas without 'personifying' or individualising the processes by which ideas are shaped, produced, changed. It emphasises that there is a history of '*mentalités collectives*', recognising the continuum between the everyday and the elite, between 'commonsense' and 'high theory'. Ideas have most meaning in their use, in the way they influence other minds and wider social processes, something which occurs by challenging and changing patterns of understanding. As well as looking at the impact of particular women of ideas, the series brings their work to a wider audience, to encourage a greater understanding of the contribution of these women to the way that we *do* think – and also the way that we perhaps *should* think – about knowledge and the human condition.

Liz Stanley

Acknowledgements

At times I was far from sure this book would ever get written. As a counsellor in higher education I am no longer continually nourished by the energy and ideas of an academic community. I miss this greatly, and so am grateful indeed for the help and support of Professor Sandra Harris of Nottingham Trent University. She organised a grant from the CRICC to pay the Counselling Service to release me to work on the book. She fought for me so that I could continue to write. I am also grateful to Liz Stanley for being so delighted when, after she had given up hope, I contacted her with the news that the book was again on its way. Her keen editorial eye shaped and guided this text at key moments. The support of Margaret Beetham and Diana Kealey, both dear and precious friends, continues to sustain me. Philippa Berry also lovingly validated my work at a time when it was hard to believe that my academic life could continue. The English Department at Trent, especially Liz Morrish, Sue Thomas, Tracey Skelton and Greg Woods, have each in their own way helped this book along, and generously offered encouragement, friendship and professional support. My fellow counsellors, especially Ivis Kennington, Marion Bennett, Billie Riley, Penny Hayman and William Hallidie Smith, in their different ways, also enabled this book to happen. The Sage editorial team encouraged the book through its various stages in a most professional and caring way.

Finally, I want to thank Adrienne Rich herself, for the time, energy and care she gave to reading and commenting on the manuscript, for checking my wilder thoughts and for filling gaps in my knowledge. In upholding against all the odds her desire for justice, and through the inspirational visionary wisdom of her thought, she has won worldwide respect. I consider myself especially privileged to have had the opportunity to read and to write about her work, and to have her letters and comments during the process of writing this book.

Abbreviations

TP	Adrienne Rich, *Time's Power: Poems 1985–1988*. New York and London: W.W. Norton, 1989.
WIFT	Adrienne Rich, *What Is Found There: Notebooks on Poetry and Politics*. New York and London: W.W. Norton, 1993.
YNL	Adrienne Rich, *Your Native Land, Your Life: Poem*s. New York and London: W.W. Norton, 1986.
YRG	bell hooks, *Yearning: Race, Gender and Cultural Politics*. London: Turnaround, 1991.

Introduction

In this short book, I have the task of introducing readers to the complex work of an internationally recognised American poet and theorist, Adrienne Rich. My aim is to explore and to make more accessible some of the ideas that have informed her writings in prose and in poetry over the last four decades. As I write in 1996, Rich is 67 and still writing – even more powerfully and ever more insightfully. I cannot hope to address the entire span of her thought in these few pages, but the more limited project, of indicating to readers what I have found fascinating in thinking about and teaching her work, is perhaps sufficient to this day.

Few women writers have had such a wide impact on contemporary feminist thought as Adrienne Rich. Her essays, emerging from within the global ferment of feminist activity, include controversial contributions to feminist theory, provocative definitions of lesbian identity, and vigorous challenges to the various institutions in and through which women have been controlled: patriarchal motherhood; the economic exploitation of corporate capitalism; the nuclear family; compulsory heterosexuality. These challenges, including her early call for women's personal and collective *experience* to become more central to the educational institution, remain contentious within academia. More recently and for very different (theoretical) reasons, a focus on women's 'experience' has been questioned within feminism also. However, it seems to me that to make women's experience an integral part of the curriculum both inside and outside Women's Studies, and to base our politics within the material and spiritual urgencies of women's lives, remains profoundly revolutionary. I would still use her essay 'Towards a Woman-Centered University' (1973–74), to introduce students to the 'outrageous', 'improbable' idea of an alternative to the 'man-centred university', that bastion of 'masculine privilege' that has dominated our education system since the Renaissance (*LSS*: 126–7). I would do so, however, in the full awareness that the Rich writing in 1996 may not be in agreement with the Rich writing in 1974. Her work continuously evolves – revolves, re-visions, re-presents itself in different terms – and is newly weighed and reassessed with each fresh twist of feminist theorising. I have found that each generation of students has been inspired anew with the desire to use their education as a key to social change: as Rich says, 'not merely for changing institutions but for human redefinition; not merely for equal rights but for a new kind of being' (*LSS*: 155). This still seems a valid enterprise to me.

Rich is a major poet: more than 15 books of poetry to date have been written over a period of 40 years. Her poetry and her prose have brought Rich high praise, a vast range of critical evaluation, and a reputation that has spread far beyond the shores of North America: indeed her work has now been translated into many languages; German, Spanish, Swedish, Dutch, Hebrew, Greek, Italian and Japanese. The jacket of her latest prose work *What is Found There* lists the following prizes, awards and fellowships: two Guggenheim Fellowships, the Fellowship of the Academy of American Poets, the Ruth Lilly Poetry Prize, the Lenore Marshall/*Nation* Prize for Poetry, the Fund for Human Dignity Award of the National Gay Task Force, the Common Wealth Award in Literature, the Lambda Book Award, the *Los Angeles Times* Book Prize for Poetry, the National Book Award, the Frost Silver Medal of the Poetry Society of America, the Elmer Jones Bobst Award of New York University, and the Poet's Prize. This is far from an exhaustive list – I have not itemised many of the awards from the sixties – and the publication of each new book adds to the honours now heaped on this once severely chastised young poet. Nadine Gordimer, not inappropriately, sees Rich's radical vision as comparable to the wisdom and philosophy of William Blake: 'In her vision of warning and her celebration of life, Adrienne Rich is the Blake of American letters'.[1] Perhaps predictably, mainstream American literary establishments have been reluctant to claim her, their responses ranging from extreme hostility to mere ambivalence – just as Rich herself is ambivalent about the honours they have now heaped upon her – but feminist voices have upheld her 'prophetic intelligence' as a radical vision which cannot be ignored.[2] It is throughout the women's movement worldwide that she is most renowned and, whether eulogised or chastised, her voice weaves itself in and through many of the multiform writings and diverse strands of feminist thought. It is rare to open a feminist book without seeing her words quoted somewhere!

Adrienne Rich was born in Baltimore, Maryland, on 16 May, 1929, on the verge of the Great Depression, 'in my father's workplace, a hospital in the Black ghetto, whose lobby contained an immense white marble statue of Christ' (*BBP*: 101). Baltimore was then a city segregating white from Black, and upheld Christian culture over that of all other religious groups. Her father, Arnold Rich, was at the time teaching and researching in the Department of Pathology at the Johns Hopkins Medical School, and was later made professor of pathology. A Jew, 'from Birmingham, Alabama, his father, Samuel, was Ashkenazic, an immigrant from Austria-Hungary and his mother, Hattie Rice, a Sephardic Jew from Vicksburg, Mississippi' (*BBP*:101). As a Jew, Arnold Rich grew up in a white southern Protestant-Christian dominated world. Recognisably Jewish, he married a woman from a white southern Protestant family. Her mother Helen and her maternal grandmother Mary Gravely were, Rich tells us, both 'frustrated artists and intellectuals, a lost writer and a lost composer between them' (*BBP*: 102). Before her marriage to Arnold, Helen had trained seriously to be a concert pianist and had won a scholarship to study at the Peabody Institute in Baltimore. Once married, she gave up the pursuit of a concert career and, though she continued composing, this was not allowed to conflict with her duties as wife and mother – not to Arnold's much desired son, but to two daughters.

The social world of Rich's childhood was southern, genteel, middle-class, white and Christian. Both the school and the church attended by Rich were Episcopalian and, 'though without belief', she was nonetheless baptised and confirmed (*BBP*: 105). Her father had 'no use for organised religion' and her mother observed the social niceties of Christianity as a matter of expedience and they were both, it appears, concerned about 'questions of social belonging and acceptability' (*BBP*: 175, 110). When Rich was married in 1953, at Hillel House, Harvard – to Alfred Conrad, an economist – her parents refused to come: 'I was marrying a Jew of the "wrong kind" from an Eastern European background' (*BBP*: 114). In the essay 'Split at the Root: An Essay on Jewish Identity' (1982), and in such poems as 'At the Jewish New Year' (1955), 'Jerusalem' (1966), 'Sources' (1981–82), 'Yom Kippur 1984' (1985), and 'Eastern War Time' (1990), her lifelong meditation on Jewish identity may be traced.

Race and racism: learning from others

Another crucial and formative experience, which was to shape Rich's thinking as a theorist and writer, can be identified from these early years. For four years she was tended and cared for by a Black nurse, from whom she learned 'a great deal about the possibilities of dignity in a degrading situation', within a culture dominated by the unwritten rules of segregation (*OWB*: 253–5). Rich tells us: 'Baltimore in the thirties and forties was a deeply segregated city. There weren't back-of-the-bus rules, but Black people did not shop in the same department stores as white people, there was the interracial eating taboo and so on. That kind of thing'. Looking back on this experience, she was to say, in the 1986 introduction to *Of Woman Born*, written for the tenth anniversary of its publication, that 'I tried to blur that relationship into the mother–daughter relationship. But a "personalised understanding" did not prevent me from gliding over the concrete system within which Black women have had to nurture the oppressor's children'.[3]

The essays 'Teaching Language in Open Admissions' (1972), and 'Disloyal to Civilisation: Feminism, Racism and Gynephobia' (1978), collected in *On Lies, Secrets and Silence*, are especially valuable for their highlighting of race and racism as crucial issues for feminists to address and mark further developments in Rich's thought.[4] Influenced by the massive direct action of the sixties – the demonstrations, the speeches, the leaflets – of the civil rights movement, Rich becomes more and more politicised. The pride, the indignation, the dignity of the Black struggle – which had grown in intensity from 1960 onward, culminating in ghetto rebellions and widespread urban riots – were to be met with brutal assaults and mass jailings, violence and fierce repression. It was a time of intense intellectual challenge and fiery ideological ferment, relentless struggles against police brutality, and sustained protest against the intransigence and hostility of whites. Throughout the decade, exclusionary practices – in law, enfranchisement, housing, employment and education – were repeatedly challenged, and even then, what legal changes were won through this massive uprising against injustice were only reluctantly conceded.

Rich had moved to New York in 1966 with the family, at a time when, increasingly, the city was in turmoil – strikes, shortages, pitched battles and middle-class paranoia were the order of the day. In the year when Martin Luther King was assassinated, Rich was being hired as a poet-teacher in the SEEK Program at City College, New York. SEEK was a basic writing programme for open admissions students, mostly Asian, Black and Puerto Rican freshmen from ghetto high schools who would not otherwise have survived either economically or academically in the higher education context. She was, she says, acting on 'a political decision to use my energies in work with "disadvantaged" (Black and Puerto Rican) students' (*LSS*: 53). I imagine Rich trawling the bookstores looking for suitable material for her teaching: 'the bookstores of the late sixties were crowded with paperbacks by Frederick Douglass, Malcolm X, Frantz Fanon, Langston Hughes, Eldridge Cleaver, W.E. DuBois' (*LSS*: 51). Toni Cade Bambara's *The Black Woman*, *The Autobiography of Malcom X* and his published speeches, *The Autobiography of Frederick Douglass*, the poetry of LeRoi Jones (later Imamu Amiri Baraka), the cultural criticism of Larry Neal (a colleague at City College) and the organising of Black feminists were all important at this pivotal moment in Rich's thinking, in contributing to the development and growth of her understanding of race and racism. Toni Cade Bambara, along with

Paul Blackburn, Robert Cumming, David Henderson and June
Jordan, were also involved in teaching remedial English to Puerto
Rican 'freshmen' from ghetto high schools in this programme. I
would suggest that a foundational insight from this experience,
which was to reverberate through the next two decades of her
commitment to feminism, was the crucial recognition that language and literature could be *'used against'* underprivileged young
men and women – 'to keep them in their place, to mystify, to bully,
to make them feel powerless' (*LSS*: 63). Learning from others different from herself is becoming a principle that underpins her
work. As we read her essays and her poetry, we find a generous,
unstinting effort: 'to carry my thoughts on feminism and racism
beyond the confines of my own mind' (*LSS*: 279).

Even when she was a child, her father had encouraged his
daughter to read widely. He had made her feel special, had trained
her to be a writer and a careful reader: the house 'full of books', his
library wide-ranging, Victorian, Pre-Raphaelite (*LSS*: 388).
Tennyson, Keats, Blake, Rossetti, Swinburne, Carlyle and Pater
were to form the basis of her early reading. Sent to an all-girls'
school, she was taught by women who cared 'about the life of the
mind', women who continued the prodding, 'the insistence that
my best could be even better', begun by her father (*LSS*: 237–8).

Rich left Baltimore to go to Radcliffe College, Cambridge,
Massachusetts, in 1947. It was then still a women's college, where
she was taught by 'great men', as she comments 25 years later. It
was plain that 'the real power and money were invested in
Harvard's institutions, from which we were excluded. Taking
classes in the Yard, working with the great (male) minds of the
Harvard faculty, were the signs of our special privilege as women'
(Rich, 1976a: 12). There she was 'trained to think like imitation
men, taught that the history, culture and norms of the world were
masculine, that to be human was masculine' (ibid.). These formative and very specific experiences at Radcliffe provided the
foundation for her devastating critique of the elitism of the literary
canon, and her invitation to women to *claim*, rather than merely to
receive their education.

Rich's contribution to feminist literary criticism

As an undergraduate, Rich was introduced to the work of Frost, Dylan Thomas, Donne, MacNeice, Stevens and Yeats. She found herself reading 'the "great" long poems of modernism: Eliot's "The Waste Land", Hart Crane's "The Bridge", Pound's "Cantos"; and later, William Carlos Williams's "Paterson", Allen Ginsberg's "Howl"' (*LSS*: 256). This early grounding in the male masters, to the virtual exclusion of even such female writers as H.D. and Emily Dickinson, was the spur driving her towards the crucial contributions to feminist criticism she was to make throughout the seventies and eighties.

In 'When We Dead Awaken: Writing as Re-Vision' (1971) Rich states what has become a foundational, much quoted principle for feminist criticism:

> Re-vision – the act of looking back, of seeing with fresh eyes, of entering an old text from a new critical direction – is for women more than a chapter in cultural history: it is an act of survival. Until we can understand the assumptions in which we are drenched we cannot know ourselves. And this drive to self-knowledge, for women, is more than a search for identity: it is part of our refusal of the self-destructiveness of male-dominated society. (*LSS*: 35)

Recognising that she had had to seek out for herself the work of Sappho, Christina Rossetti, Emily Dickinson, Elinor Wylie, Edna Millay and H.D., Rich spoke passionately for the necessity for women to create an alternative to the male-stream canon, thus contributing to a major and energetic debate around the reclamation of 'lost' women authors in history and literature (*LSS*: 39). Rich draws attention to those 'feminist scholars, teachers and graduate students, joined by feminist writers, editors, and publishers, [who] have for a decade been creating more subversive occasions, challenging the sacredness of the gentlemanly canon' (*LSS*: 33). As she wryly phrased it: 'when you read or hear about "great issues," "major texts," "the mainstream of Western Thought," you are hearing about what men, above all white men, in their male subjectivity, have decided is important' (*LSS*: 232). In her headnotes to 'When We Dead Awaken', Rich launches this wide-ranging attack on the MLA (Modern Language Association of America) convention,

characterising its activities as a '"procession of the sons of educated men" (Virginia Woolf): a congeries of old-boys' networks,
academicians rehearsing their numb canons in sessions dedicated
to the literature of white males, junior scholars under the lash of
"publish or perish" delivering papers in the bizarrely lit drawing-
rooms of immense hotels: a ritual competition veering between
cynicism and desperation' (*LSS*: 33). Charles B. Harris, quoting the
above passage from *On Lies, Secrets and Silence*, notes that 'scant
attention' was paid to feminist theory and criticism in 1978, but 'in
the 1994 program over a third of the convention sessions listed
under "Literary Criticism and Theory" focus on questions of
gender and race; no fewer than seven deal directly with gay and
lesbian theory. Similar concerns with feminism, race, gender, and
power relations pervade the rest of the Program' (Harris, 1996: 22).
Of course Harris is remarking on a huge paradigm shift within
Literary Studies, from an emphasis on canonical studies to a wide-
ranging analysis of the workings of power within culture, but
clearly Rich's critique did not go unnoticed.

Indeed, her powerful critical assessment was to inspire the new
field of Feminist Literary Studies, and lent force to the creation of
a new model for critical enquiry which was to bring race, gender,
class and feminism from the margins to the centre of literary
endeavour: Rich was to inspire feminist critics to redraw the boundaries of the discipline. Rachel Blau DuPlessis here picks up on
Rich's challenge to 'the social practices and mental structures that
repress women,' in articulating her sense of this major re-visionary
effort: 'To construct her new consciousness, the woman must at
one and the same time sever her allegiance to the destructive
views of the past and transcend the presence of destructive
ideologies in herself, producing that critique distinctive of twenti-
eth-century women writers "not to pass on a tradition, but to break
its hold over us"' (Blau DuPlessis, 1985: 127).

Feminist critics were to set to work eagerly around this task of
retrieval and re-vision, researching and reappraising female literary heritages.[5] It was soon recognised that women writers and
readers do bring different perceptions, assumptions and expectations to their appreciation of texts. Elaine Showalter was to
comment: 'Feminism spoke to our lived and our literary experience

with the fierce urgency of a revelation or a Great Awakening' (1985: 5). She quoted Sandra Gilbert, whose excited words give some indication of the import of Rich's foundational precept for feminist criticism: 'most feminist critics speak . . . like people who must bear witness, people who must enact and express in their own lives and words the revisionary sense of transformation that seems inevitably to attend the apparently simple discovery that the experiences of women in and with literature are different from those of men' (Gilbert, 1979: 850). The excitement of these years gathers to it a legendary quality: 'It was an intellectual revolution, charged with the excitement of violating existing paradigms and discovering a new field of vision' (Showalter, 1985: 5). The project of making women's experience visible was to expose a multitude of repressive mechanisms in force within the field of academia and, according to Joan W. Scott, this enabled feminist analysis: 'to unmask all claims to objectivity as an ideological cover for masculine bias by pointing out the shortcomings, incompleteness, and exclusiveness of "mainstream history"' (Butler and Scott, 1992: 30). Ultimately, the authority of experience as the origin of knowledge was itself to come under fire as feminist critics begin to problematise and to re-envision 'experience' in response to questions raised within post-structuralist theory just as, more recently, academicians in the US find themselves calling for a reinstatement of a canon, in the face of universities' weakening commitment to literary studies.[6] These developments do not, however, invalidate the crucial contribution made by Rich, in her groundbreaking 1971 essay.

Creating theory out of experience

It is interesting to chart the development of her ideas around 'experience' from the early formative period of Rich's work. If the thirties had been 'a decade of economic desperation, social unrest, war, and also of affirmed political art', by the fifties and sixties the context for producing art had changed utterly (*BBP*: 171–2). In this extract from 'Blood, Bread and Poetry', she looks back to the thirties, forties and fifties with a keen political appreciation of the social and political forces shaping these decades. The thirties were receding behind the fogs of the Cold War, the selling of the nuclear family with the mother at home as its core, heightened activity by the FBI and CIA, a retreat by many artists from so-called 'protest' art, witch-hunting among artists and intellectuals as well as in the State Department, anti-Semitism, scapegoating of homosexual men and lesbians, and with a symbolic victory for the Cold War crusade in the 1953 electrocution of Ethel and Julius Rosenberg. (*BBP*: 171)

An increasingly dangerous world for the artist and intellectual had compelled a retreat from politically committed art. But at Harvard, Rich was taught by a socialist gay man, Francis Otto Matthiessen, who refused to exclude the events in the outside world from classroom textual criticism. Rather than being taught text-focused New Critical theory, Rich was brought to an understanding of the political conditions and historical currents of the wider world. With Matthiessen, Rich encountered Blake, Keats, Byron, Yeats, Stevens – if not against a historical context, then never 'in the realm of pure textual criticism'. Searching for 'some clue or key to life', she also finds the work of Mary Wollstonecraft, Simone de Beauvoir and James Baldwin, writers who helped her to realise this foundational principle of her art – 'that what had seemed simply "the way things are" could actually be a social construct, advantageous to some people and detrimental to others, and that these constructs could be criticised and changed' (*BBP*: 176). The territories of gender, race and power could be identified and mapped, and were not simply 'part of my private turmoil, a secret misery, an individual failure'.

Rich creates an art out of lived experience and accepts that language is a social construct

Even as early as 1956, Rich dates her poems by year. This early acknowledgement of the interdependence of art and life, of art and history, of poetry and experience, will be developed through the coming decades: 'It was a declaration that placed poetry in a historical continuity, not above, or outside history' (*BBP*: 180). Thus begins a lifelong allegiance to a poetry (and later, a theory) emerging out of lived experience – the actuality of personal, social and historical experience becomes both 'source and resource' for the work (*ARP*: xii). Catherine Stimpson, who amusingly characterises Rich's worried opponents as muttering darkly of deconstruction and the sign, highlights and celebrates Rich's resistance to post-structuralism in the interests of pursuing a materialist politics:

> *Surely*, they whisper nervously, she must know about our post-structural awareness of the nature of the sign. *Surely*, she must realise that language is a fiction, not a transparent vehicle of truth. . . . *Surely*, she must now admit that this system creates the human subject, not the other way round. (Stimpson, 1988: 141)

It is clear from her recommitment to 'writing the body' in 'Notes toward a Politics of Location' (1984), (a talk for the First Summer School of Critical Semiotics, Conference on 'Women, Feminist Identity and Society', which was held in Utrecht, Holland) that, yes, she does know about post-structuralism, and no, she unrepentantly locates herself as engaged in a struggle for political accountability and responsibility within theory. Despite her clear recognition that language is a social construct, she returns to the material to 'Pick up again the long struggle against lofty and privileged abstraction' as the core of revolutionary process (*BBP*: 213). In these notes she launches her Marxist-influenced critique of 'free floating abstraction', of theory 'severed from the doings of living people', of theory that is dislocated – abstracted – from time and space and history.

Locating my self in my body: self-scrutiny as a methodology

Identifying the specificities of 'bodies' is necessary if women are to work towards a society 'without domination', but those specificities carry more complexities of meaning than any mere essentialist notion of the female body: 'To locate myself in my body means more than understanding what it has meant to me to have a vulva and clitoris and uterus and breasts. It means recognizing this white skin, the places it has taken me, the places it has not let me go' (*BBP*: 215–16).

The emphasis on race, history and experience within the sexed body threads its way through many essays from the early seventies on.[7] But it is in *Of Woman Born* that Rich truly begins in her prose to fuse the feminist commitment to the ground of experience, in developing a mode of representation embodying the principle that the personal is political. In her poetry she had long recognised the need to identify 'her relationship to atrocities and injustice, the sources of her pain, fear and anger, the meaning of her resistance', but now she risks her own deeply personal voice in speaking of the anger and tenderness at the core of her experience of mothering (*LSS*: 251). As Barbara Gelpi and Albert Gelpi point out, in *Adrienne Rich's Poetry and Prose*, their invaluable collection of reviews and criticism of Rich's work,

> The most difficult but at the same time the most liberating aspect of this re-vision is that it involves the constant reassessment of the ways in which one has participated, whatever one's race, gender or class, in one's own oppression. This focused and healing self-scrutiny so char-acteristic of Rich, so much the ground of her poetry's fused insights and of her prose analysis, has also been her central, though by no means her single, contribution to the methodology at the core of all feminist theorizing. (*ARP*: xii)

Throughout her work, she has sought to make connections among the contradictory events of her own life to illuminate women's experiences of powerlessness, and to forge the politics and inspire the activism needed to counter multiform situations of oppression. She urges women 'to create a language and worldview of our own, to perceive the vast landscape of woman-hating and male envy of women, underlying the haze of heterosexual romance, the domestic idyll, and the jargon of "pathology" and "deviance"' (*ARP*: 253).

Language as transforming power

Her re-visionary work of critique of culture and ideology, which is both theoretical and poetic, brings Rich to consider the part played by language within sexually related power dynamics: its prescriptive force, the categories that define and organise our realities, its power to mediate and thus change how we perceive our experience. In

'Power and Danger: Works of a Common Woman' (1977), Rich points to the language we articulate, and which articulates us, as being a concrete and material resource having 'transforming power':

> When we become acutely, disturbingly aware of the language we are using and that is using us, we begin to grasp a material resource that women have never before collectively attempted to repossess. . . . Language is as real, as tangible in our lives as streets, pipelines, telephone switchboards, microwaves, radioactivity, cloning laboratories, nuclear power stations . . . as long as our language is inadequate, our vision remains formless, our thinking and feeling are still running in the old cycles, our process may be 'revolutionary' but not transformative. (*LSS*: 247)

If language mediates reality and reality is something else apart from the words and images we use to describe it, then every myth, every history, every reality, may be mediated anew. Myths may be re-envisioned, reinterpreted, rewritten, re-presented. Denaturalising the terms of patriarchal language is not enough, destabilising inherited patterns of gendered signification is not enough: it is not enough to repudiate the social and legal scripts; the political systems; the cultural codes and conventions; the religious rules, the rituals – they must be transformed, rewritten, lived according to a different script. Rich's radical feminist, woman-centred poetry begins to formulate restitutive re-visionary mythologies embodying more than a refusal to collaborate with the dominant masculine ideology, language and law of the heterosexual imperative. The effort of the poetry becomes directed towards producing strategic re-visionary fictions in which Rich attempts to grasp the specificity and integrity of living in a female body – I understand her at this stage as seeing biological difference in contrary rather than oppositional terms, and as exploring in both poetry and prose the multiplicity, ambiguity and heterogeneity of woman-centred perspectives in their difference from those created by men. In *Of Woman Born*, Rich argues for a grounding of that perspective, in writing of the female body as an available material resource for an expanding consciousness:

> female biology . . . has far more radical implications than we have yet come to appreciate. Patriarchal thought has limited female biology to its

own narrow specifications. The feminist vision has recoiled from female biology for these reasons; it will, I believe, come to view our physicality as a resource, rather than a destiny. In order to live a fully human life we require not only *control* of our bodies (though control is a prerequisite); we must touch the unity and resonance of our physicality, our bond with the natural order, the corporeal ground of our intelligence. (*OWB*: 39)

This stance was to call forth a chorus of critical condemnation. Elaine Showalter, in her important essay 'Feminist Criticism in the Wilderness', saw Rich's emphasis on 'confession' and the body as 'cruelly prescriptive. There is a sense in which the exhibition of bloody wounds becomes an initiation ritual quite separate and disconnected from critical insight' (Showalter, 1985: 252). And certainly Rich risks the charge that this woman-centred perspective 'was not to place women at the centre of culture and society, but to recapitulate, and in some sense to accept, the formulation of woman as Other, the very category of being against which Simone de Beauvoir had originally rebelled' (Eisenstein, 1984: 135).

Back to the body: essentialism and the political task

Many saw this strategy as biologistic, as essentialist, unhelpful to the cause – but how far is writing which explores female specificity to be condemned? To Hester Eisenstein, 'the view of woman as an eternal "essence" represented a retreat from the fundamentally liberating concept of woman as agent, actor, and subject, rather than object' (1984: 135). And yet, as Diana Fuss has suggested, 'essentialism can be deployed effectively in the service of both idealist and materialist, progressive and reactionary, mythologising and resistive discourses' (Fuss, 1989: xii).[8] But of course, the conceptualisation of our own bodies is not some kind of fixed absolute but a construct that is being continually reformulated, and whose meanings may, for well or ill, be culturally engendered. As Rosi Braidotti suggests in her astute and important essay, 'The Politics of Ontological Difference':

one should start politically with the assertion of the need for the presence of real-life women in positions of discursive subjecthood, and theoretically with the recognition of the primacy of the bodily roots of subjectivity, rejecting both the traditional vision of the subject as universal, neutral, or gender-free and the binary logic that sustains it. (Braidotti, 1989: 90)

The female body is always already mediated in and through language. How we understand our bodies is continually being shaped within the psychical and social meanings circulating in culture, just as our view of ourselves is constructed in relation to specific familial, temporal and geographic contexts. We all may internalise disparaging and harassing myths and messages to our continuing distress. However, 'the body' as such is far from being a conception 'beyond the reaches of historical change, immutable and consequently outside the field of political intervention' (ibid.: 92–3). To take such a view is itself ultimately reductive and deterministic in that it refuses the very possibility of political intervention. In Braidotti's words: 'a feminist woman theoretician who is interested in thinking about sexual differences and the feminine today cannot afford not to be essentialist'. Neither can women afford to disembody sexual difference in any project concerned with female subjectivity. As the 'threshold of subjectivity' and 'the point of intersection, as the interface between the biological and the social', the body is the site or location for the construction of the subject in relation to other subjects (ibid.: 97). Rich was drawn to the body of woman to formulate her strategic response to misogyny with what Braidotti was later to call 'the positive project of turning difference into a strength, of affirming its positivity' (ibid.: 101). Rich later withdrew from this trajectory of her thought but, as this contemplation within theory shows, she could have trusted the intelligence of her earlier political instincts, after all.

On lesbian identity and difference

Difference, of course, entails more than the differences between male and female; it refers also to 'differences *among* women: differences of class, race and sexual preference for which the signifier "woman" is inadequate as a blanket term' (Braidotti,

1989: 93). Questions around identity and difference – sexual difference – racial difference, religious difference – come to the fore in the mid-seventies. Speaking at the Modern Language Association in 1976, at a panel convened by the Women's Commission and the Gay Caucus, with co-panellists June Jordan, Audre Lorde and Honor Moore, Rich presented her controversial paper 'It Is the Lesbian in Us' (1976), followed a year later by 'The Meaning of Our Love for Women Is What We Have Constantly to Expand' (1977), a talk given to a small group of Gay Pride demonstrators who had separated themselves off to hold their own rally. These essays, together with *The Dream of a Common Language: Poems 1974–77*, publicly mark Rich's coming out as lesbian.[9] Rich describes reading Judy Grahn's poem, 'A Woman Is Talking to Death', in 1974, and tells us of her coming to consciousness as lesbian:

> Something the poem had unlocked in me was the audacity of loving women, the audacity of claiming a stigmatised desire, the audacity to resist the temptations to abandon or betray or deny 'all of our lovers' – those of whatever sex, color, class with whom we need to make common cause and who need us. 'A Woman Is Talking to Death' was a boundary-breaking poem for me: it exploded both desire and politics. (*WIFT*: 172)

Desire and politics: two crucial terms in any consideration of what it means to claim an 'unspeakable' lesbian identity (*LSS*: 199).[10] To come out; to accept and affirm that self-chosen desire against enormous odds is to break through internalised homophobia to a point where self-acceptance is possible. To then identify the 'complex, demanding realm of linguistic and relational distinctions' that constitute lesbian identity; to eschew any collaboration with secrets, denial, silence, omission, veiling, erasure, *lying*; to 'grasp' our experience in words spoken publicly; to theorise from that experience so as to create a politically aware community of resistance, and to set all that against a culture that stigmatises love between women – is both daunting and exhilarating, dangerous and necessary to survival (*LSS*: 202).

The transformation of silence into language and action

Again, a panel sponsored by the Women's Commission and the Gay Caucus of the MLA provides the context for a crucial meeting of minds: this time Julia P. Stanley, Mary Daly, Audre Lorde, Judith McDaniel and Adrienne Rich speak on the topic: 'The Transformation of Silence into Language and Action', and produce a collection of papers later published in *Sinister Wisdom*, in summer 1978 (*LSS*: 275). Lesbian identity politics rests on the definitional 'coming out' moment, the transpositional movement into presence – into visibility, into language, and thus into cultural intelligibility – of the formerly nameless, the invisible, the silent. Yet the term 'lesbian', though it claims to include all lesbians, remains exclusive: it promises full disclosure, and at the same time is not all, for what can lesbians be said to share? Who decides what constitutes 'lesbian' as a category? As Judith Butler comments, 'the locus of opacity has shifted: before, you did not know whether I "am," but now you do not know what that means . . .' (Butler, 1991: 15–16). On what basis do lesbians create a community, a politics – what common element, what specificity determines the claim to lesbian identity? Is it a particular mode of eroticism? 'Is it the *specificity* of a lesbian experience or lesbian desire or lesbian sexuality that lesbian theory needs to elucidate?' (ibid.: 17). There is, of course, no necessary commonality between lesbians and this was already clear at this MLA conference, where Rich urges the breaking of another silence, that between Black and white feminists. Her vision of bonding across a problematic difference required that lesbians begin to speak of the bitter, painful or oblique connections between white and Black women. Indeed, such encounters did take place, very painfully, between Black, white, Afro-Caribbean, Hispanic, Chicana, Gentile, Jew, Christian, heterosexual, lesbian, old, young – in which grievances were aired and differences, sometimes destructively, engaged with.

'Compulsory Heterosexuality and Lesbian Existence' (1980) was written on request for a special 'Sexuality' issue of the scholarly feminist journal *Signs*, with the aim of combating the erasure of lesbian existence 'from scholarly feminist literature' and to 'encourage heterosexual feminists to examine heterosexuality as a political institution' (*BBP*: 23). It was heavily criticised for its notion of a lesbian continuum, predominantly being seen as denying lesbians any sexual specificity. It was clearly an impulse towards creating bridges between women – but it is rarely praised for its major contribution in providing lesbian and gay theory with a powerful critique of heterosexuality as an institution, as that which 'sets itself up as the original, the true, the authentic; the norm that determines the real' (Butler, 1991: 20). It is clear, however, that this essay again provoked argument and debate throughout the women's movement, challenging women as always to reach for a radical complexity out beyond themselves.

A strong activist emphasis on 'historical responsibility' is evident from the early to mid-eighties on (*BBP*: 137). An important essay from this period is 'Living the Revolution' (1986), in which Rich deeply engages with the work of Russian Jewish writer Raya Dunayevskaya, 'a major thinker in the history of Marxism and of women's liberation – one of the longest continuously active woman revolutionaries of the twentieth century' (Rich, 1986: 3).[11] She weighs and assesses anew what Dunayevskaya had called 'Marx's humanism', which she saw 'not as a *turning backward* but as a rescuing for the present a legacy she saw as . . . having been diminished, distorted and betrayed'.[12] She herself returns to reread Marx's *The German Ideology*, and in so doing, reaffirms her profound awareness of the necessity 'to keep defining and describing our relationship both to capitalism and to socialism, and to talk seriously about our place in the interconnecting movements for bread, self-determination, dignity and justice' (*BBP*: 159).

Amid the increasingly right-wing political and religious ethos of the eighties in the US, and the growing ruthlessness of corporate power worldwide, Rich develops further the awareness of 'her art's responsive and responsible relationship to history' (*WIFT*: xiv). She re-examines the political role of the poet/activist in *What is Found There*, exploring the complexities of the relation of the artist to revolutionary movement and, critical of the poetry of 'resigned interiority', urges a 'truly revolutionary art . . . through which waste, greed, brutality, frozen indifference, "blind sorrow," and anger are transmuted into some drenching recognition of the "*What if* "? – the possible' (*WIFT*: 233, 241).

Though Rich would identify herself primarily as a poet, rather than an essayist or theorist, an analysis of the poetry is not the primary purpose of this book. Overall, I seek to elucidate and expand on many of the critical arguments within feminism in so far as they relate to Rich's work. I do, however, sometimes refer to the poetry, for this is frequently where ideas initially develop and insights are formulated which later become articulated in her theoretical essays. (It is with some regret that an extended analysis of 'The Twenty-One Love Poems' and many other important poems was cut from the original manuscript for this book, in order to limit its cost to readers. Hopefully, this work will eventually be published elsewhere.) Chapter 1 explores the beginnings of her feminist identification as it emerges in the early poetry, and seeks to highlight a few of the major themes that are to come in the later work. Chapter 2 charts the influence of the political protests of the sixties, the birth of the radical feminist movement and the identification of patriarchy as the oppressing structure of male domination. For Rich, the apparent congruence of sex and violence in the male psyche add fury to the poems of this era. Chapter 3 takes as its focus *Of Woman Born*, and points readers towards Rich's critique of abstraction, her long-standing antipathy to dualistic thought forms, and her focus on experience as a foundational principle for her radical feminism. Holistically fusing the socio-political with the psycho-spiritual, she deplores the forceful regulation of women's bodies within the institution of mothering and, influenced by writings within the new women's spirituality movement, embarks on a journey through anthropology to find alternatives to the white male god of patriarchal religious forms. Chapter 4 explores her politically motivated attempt to rethink the heterosexual–lesbian difference into a continuum in 'Compulsory Heterosexuality and Lesbian Existence' (1980). The struggle to develop an integrated analysis and a practice based on the fact that the major systems of oppression interlock with each other, brings Rich to appreciate the political necessity for 'diversity' and a commitment to 'radical complexity'. Negotiating the differences between women involves a reluctance to foreclose the questions posed by real material

existence and the body. Chapter 5 sees Rich again powerfully influenced by the writings of men and women of colour and determined
to expose the exclusions perpetrated by a white bourgeois feminist
movement. Turning away from the universalising identity politics
of radical feminism towards Marx's humanism in *Blood, Bread and
Poetry*, Rich formulates her groundbreaking politics of location.
Bringing the abstractions of (?post-structuralist) theory 'back
down to earth again', Rich affirms her self-consciously historical,
fully accountable analysis of power relations in the real world
(*BBP*: 219).

Chapter 6 identifies the return to sources, home and her Jewish
inheritance, of *Sources*, and 'Split at the Root: An Essay on Jewish
Identity' (1982), indicating how imperative it is to combat anti-
Semitism and, following her move to California, identifying the
otherness of cultural displacement. She explores the logic of limits
and yet again reconfigures the conceptual grounding of her political commitment. Strategic outsiderhood can no longer be a viable
political stance and, somewhat paradoxically, Rich has now become
a distinguished poet of America, acknowledged as 'great' and
deeply respected even within the mainstream of American literary
life.

Notes

1 Jacket of *What is Found There: Notebooks on Poetry and Politics*. 'The clear-eyed
depth and the visionary stretch of these notes bespeak an irresistible, prophetic
intelligence and a huge heart wrestling with the transformative power of poetry up
against the needs of an emerging new world' – June Jordan.

2 On reading my script, Rich commented, somewhat wryly, 'I think of Woolf's
phrase about her reviewers' "struggle to combine respect and loathing . . ."'

3 'Ten Years Later: A New Introduction' (*OWB*: xxv). Rich also notes that
'Moreover, relying on ready-to-hand Greek mythology, I was led to generalise that
"the cathexis between mother and daughter" was endangered always and everywhere. A consideration of American Indian, African, and Afro-American myth and
philosophy might have suggested other patterns.'

4 'Teaching Language in Open Admissions', 1972 (*LSS*: 51–68). See also
'Claiming an Education', 1977 (*LSS*: 230–5).

'Disloyal to Civilisation: Feminism, Racism, Gynephobia', 1978 (*LSS*: 275–310),
takes up the themes of forging a unity between Black and white feminists in making

a commitment to 'a profound transformation of world society and of human relationships' (p.279), and the difficult question of white feminist racism within the movement: 'white feminists today, raised white in a racist society, are often ridden with *white solipsism* – not the consciously held *belief* that one race is inherently superior to all others, but a tunnel-vision which simply does not see non-white experience or existence as precious or significant, unless in spasmodic, impotent guilt-reflexes, which have little or no long-term, continuing momentum or political usefulness' (p. 306).

5 Key critics in this debate were Ellen Moers, Elaine Showalter, Sandra Gilbert, Susan Gubar, Caroline Hielbrun and Annette Kolodny. Bonnie Zimmerman took up the cause for lesbian criticism, Barbara Smith for Black criticism. Many of their important essays were collected in Showalter (1985).

6 With this paradigm shift, what was 'literature' has diversified into the study of popular culture, cinema, television, magazines and communication technology. J. Hillis Miller predicts that 'it will be hard to keep the humanities from becoming vestigial, from becoming no more than an assembly of programs that teach the communication skills needed by educated technocrats in the service of transnational corporations' (Miller, 1996: 33).

7 'Toward a Woman-Centred University', 1973–74 (*LSS*); 'Resisting Amnesia: History and Personal Life', 1983 (*BBP*); 'History stops for no-one', 1993 (*WIFT*).

8. Fuss sees essentialism as 'typically defined in opposition to difference; the doctrine of essence is viewed as precisely that which seeks to deny or to annul the very radicality of difference. The opposition is a helpful one in that it reminds us that a complex system of cultural, social, psychical, and historical differences, and not a set of pre-existent human essences, position and constitute the subject.'

9 Michelle Cliff and Adrienne Rich jointly edited *Sinister Wisdom*, a lesbian feminist journal, from 1981 to 1983.

10 'Whatever is unnamed, undepicted in images, whatever is omitted from biography, censored in collections of letters, whatever is misnamed as something else, made difficult-to-come-by, whatever is buried in the memory by the collapse of meaning under an inadequate or lying language – this will become, not merely unspoken, but *unspeakable*.'

11 See also Foreword by Adrienne Rich, to *Rosa Luxemburg, Women's Liberation, and Marx's Philosophy of Revolution*. Urbana and Chicago: University of Illinois Press, 1991: xi–xx, p. xi.

12 Foreword, ibid: xii.

1 'What I Know, I Know through Making Poems'

Feminist Beginnings in the Early Poetry[1]

> A poem can't free us from the struggle for existence, but it can uncover desires and appetites buried under the accumulating emergencies of our lives, the fabricated wants and needs we have had urged on us, have accepted as our own. It's not a philosophical or a psychological blueprint; it's an instrument for embodied experience. But we seek that experience, or recognize it when it is offered to us, because it reminds us in some way of our need. After that rearousal of desire, the task of acting on that truth, or making love, or meeting other needs, is ours.[2]
>
> Adrienne Rich (*WIFT*: 12–13)

Writing poetry above all involves a willingness to let the unconscious speak – a willingness to listen within for the whispers that tell of what we know, even though what we know may be unacceptable to us and, sometimes, because we may not want to hear, the whispers may be virtually inaudible. But to write poetry is to listen and watch for significant images, to make audible the inner whisperings, to reach deeper inward for those subtle intuitions, sensings, images, which can be released from the unconscious mind through the creativity of writing. In this way, a writer may come to know her deeper self, below the surface of the words. Poetry can be a means to access suppressed recognitions, a way to explore difficult understandings which might otherwise be buffeted out of consciousness through the fear-laden processes of repression – through avoidance, denial, forgetting. At the same time, the formal containment of poetry can serve as a way of limiting the impact of those understandings, of covering over the splits and contradictions of the life. Poetry is a technically controlled and fictional art form which can, through the intellectual clarity and the creative artifice of the poet, offer a delusory sense of harmony, completeness and perfection of order. This image of perfection may bear little relation to the struggling, self-divided real woman, the poet. Rich comments in 1964 of her earliest work, 'that these poems . . . were queerly limited; that in many cases I had suppressed, omitted, falsified even, certain disturbing elements, to gain that perfection of order' (*ARP*: 165). Yet Rich does capture something of the woman's struggle in these poems and so in this chapter I seek to identify what I see as a prescient feminism articulating itself almost against the grain of this stylised poetry.

On gatekeeping and feminism: the struggle to speak

Elegance, evasion, reserve and decorum mark Rich's poised and dignified early poems, and looking back it hardly seems surprising that W.H. Auden patronisingly faint-praised them as poems that are 'neatly and modestly dressed, speak quietly but do not mumble, respect their elders but are not cowed by them, and do not tell fibs' (*ARP*: 278). Rich was to comment, years later, in *What is Found There*, that 'If anything, I cherished a secret grudge against Auden – not because he didn't proclaim me a genius, but because he proclaimed so diminished a scope for poetry, including mine' (*WIFT*: 191). Certainly his very fifties respect for the achievements of the great modern masters had led Auden to expect a young poet to be modest and respectful towards these illustrious elders, but I would suggest that Auden's remarks also say as much about his male-centred desire for young female poets to be subservient and respectful (to him, as to the establishment) as they do about the cultural mores dominating the fifties. And, indeed, the opinion of the critic and the reviewer, especially one so eminent as Auden, is crucial to a young poet trying to make a name for herself, as these people have the power to act as gatekeepers to success. Surely the nascent feminist in Rich could not rest easy with such a verdict, one which, though it acknowledged the struggle for honesty in the poems, saw her work as gowned in modest, sweet femininity? These mores expected women to deny their own power – and offer a view of woman utterly at odds with the sense of aggressive power and virile ego-strength that Rich was by then experiencing within her female self:

> when I was in my twenties especially, I was going through a very sort of female thing – of trying to distinguish between the ego that is capable of writing poems, and then this other kind of being that you're asked to be if you're a woman, who is, in a sense, denying that ego. I had great feelings of split about that for many years actually, and there are a lot of poems I couldn't write even, because I didn't want to confess to having that much aggression, that much ego, that much sense of myself. ('Talking . . .: 31)

Something of that split can be discerned in this extract from 'Aunt Jennifer's Tigers', a poem in which the female energy and power to create is celebrated, and the feminine woman's life – of constraint, fear, subjection – is mourned:

> Aunt Jennifer's tigers prance across a screen,
> Bright topaz denizens of a world of green.
> They do not fear the men beneath the tree;
> They pace in sleek chivalric certainty.
>
> Aunt Jennifer's fingers fluttering through her wool
> Find even the ivory needle hard to pull.
> The massive weight of Uncle's wedding band
> Sits heavily upon Aunt Jennifer's hand. (*CEP*: 4)

Ironic awareness of Aunt Jennifer's position as a married woman shows her as 'ringed with ordeals she was mastered by', an image Rich sets against the 'proud and unafraid' tigers, potently and aggressively themselves, as a symbolic expression of the confident and capable female artist certain of her powers. Yet, powerful as they are, they are fixed and framed within the screen, as within the art form – static as an emblem, boundaried in space, suspended in time and utterly unfree to act in the world – just as the feminine woman, ornamental and decorative object of male domination is caged, her energy restricted, within a patriarchal culture. Aunt Jennifer 'was a person as distinct from myself as possible', but here we catch a startling glimpse of the insights which would fuel the feminist fury of later writings: 'poems are like dreams: in them you put what you don't know you know' (*LSS*: 40).

Glimpsing the future: identifying the tensions within

Readers of Rich's poetry are time and again struck by these glimpses of the feminist to come, those sometimes startling moments when she seems to anticipate the woman-centred vision of her work in the seventies. The insightful poem, 'An Unsaid Word', was included in her very first book of poetry, *A Change of World* (1951), which was published when she was 22 (*CEP*: 28). In that poem, a close to feminist voice points to the difficult tension in the woman for whom the social expectation is that she will learn to stand and wait for 'her man'. Rich, even at this stage, points to the anomaly that she is expected to let the man take the space to be alone and free, immersed in his own thoughts, despite struggling with herself and her own unmet needs, and wait patiently until 'his thoughts to her return':

> She who has power to call her man
> From that estranged intensity
> Where his mind forages alone,
> Yet keeps her peace and leaves him free,
> And when his thoughts to her return
> Stands where he left her, still his own,
> Knows this the hardest thing to learn.

Rich's poem shows awareness of the woman's position, and speaks from a womanly identification with the feeling expressed, but the further feminist question – is this right? – remains unasked: this is how it is, in 1951.

Celebrating women's history

The theme of women who wait is also explored in 'Mathilde in Normandy' (also 1951), a poem about the weaving of the Bayeux Tapestry, in which the collective handiwork of the women is upheld as more lasting than the war-making of the men (*CEP*: 29). The poet's concern is for the women, who could not know that their 'patient handiwork' would be historically important:

> ... That this should prove
> More than the personal episode, more than all
> The little lives sketched on the teeming loom
> Was then withheld from you

In this poem, Rich challenges the trivialising assumptions handed down through the centuries, that the tapestry was, in Marianne Welchel's words, 'woven as a pleasant pastime by ladies whose lords had deserted them for the world's real business, war' (Welchel, 1984: 52). As Welchel suggests, Rich's later concern with women's history, her critique of war, the importance of women's work and her celebration of women's achievements in work, in art and in history, are all prefigured here.

The lesbian in her

But not only feminist concerns are prefigured in this early poetry. I would not have known, except that Rich herself identifies it as such, that 'Stepping Backward' was a 'very guarded, carefully-wrought poem' that deals with a relationship with a woman (Bulkin, 1977: 64):

> You asked me once, and I could give no answer,
> How far dare we throw off the daily ruse,
> Official treacheries of face and name,
> Have out our true identity? (*CEP*: 32)

This farewell to a woman Rich was close to in her teens, 'and whom I really fled from – I fled from my feelings about her', shows Rich striving and yet unable to come to terms with feelings that were so socially unacceptable that they must be contained and subdued by this very intellectualised and distanced form. At the same time, this mode of concealment made it possible for Rich to publish the poem, in the intensely homophobic fifties – a period marked by scapegoating of homosexual men and lesbians, increased activity by the FBI and CIA, and witch-hunting of artists and intellectuals – because 'it could have been written to anybody'. Rich's public lesbian identification was not to come until 1975 with the publication of Elly Bulkin and Joan Larkin's anthology, *Amazon Poetry*, but as this poem shows, feelings that are unacceptable to the conscious mind, however displaced and disguised, and however laden with the pressure and urgency of thwarted desire, can emerge within the poem: 'How far dare we throw off the daily ruse . . . Have out our true identity?' (*CEP*: 32) The lesbian inflection of these lines can be concealed from the public as from the critics, and whatever 'treacheries of face and name', whatever painful losses of integrity the women's 'true identity' has suffered can, through this self-imposed (as well as culturally imposed) silencing, be displaced from consciousness and ultimately repressed.

Oppressive containment: marriage in the fifties

The tensions of a wife bound by a conventional marriage are explored in 'Autumn Equinox' (1955; in *CEP*: 95). This poem was written while Rich was an undergraduate, but by the time it was published, in 1955, Rich was actually a faculty wife at Harvard University. Of her own time at Radcliffe, Rich comments that Radcliffe women were 'receiving an insidious double message: a) You are the most privileged women in America and b) You will, of course, give your energies to ambitious and brilliant men' (Rich, 1976a: 12). In the poem, a faculty wife in middle age looks back in wistful regret, raking over the fallen leaves of a life spent in a well-worn routine of domestic activity. The poem explores the wife's sense of loss, pointing to her disillusionment with the persuasive rhetoric of romantic love, and shows her youthful dissatisfactions as giving way to a resigned old age in which the couple 'sleep as calmly as the dead'. Images of fixity and enclosure convey a graphic sense of the oppressive containment of the marriage. Recalling her wedding day, the wife remembers being 'correct and terrified' and, holding to tradition, 'Wearing the lace my mother wore before me / And buttoned shoes that pinched'. Pictures freeze this idealised moment into 'the semblance of a bride and groom / Static as figures on a mantelpiece'. Steel engravings 'Framed in black oak' contain the world, 'priggishly enclosing in a room / The marvels of the world'. The wife bites her fingers, quells her rebellion, but changing the curtains hardly changes the world. Romantic love, marriage, youthful idealism ultimately lead to this cramped life of cohabiting solitude in which the woman's world is restricted to the microcosm of the house. The wife despairs: 'I thought that life was different than it is'. Significantly, she is shown as not able to tell the uncomprehending husband of the distress she feels: thinking herself 'crazy', she refuses to listen to the whispers. In shame, she denies what she knows and what she knows becomes silenced, eventually forgotten, repressed as unacceptable. It becomes an unacknowledged lack: she does not explore the contradictions of her situation, she does not question her dissatisfactions, and ultimately sinks into the sleep that is death. The wife tries to be fulfilled, for society expects her to be. We see clearly in this poem how the free and unconstrained girl becomes the self-abnegating wife. Rich is here voicing concerns that will increasingly be aired by feminists in the next decades. Here's Jessie Bernard writing 'The Paradox of the Happy Marriage' in 1968 and asking,

> Could it be that because married women thus conform and adjust to the demands of marriage, at whatever cost to themselves, they therefore judge themselves to be happy? Are they confusing adjustment with happiness? . . . The talented woman who as a girl dreamed of becoming a singer, a dancer, actress, author, musician, nurse, even doctor, lawyer, merchant, or chief may look back with tender, secret nostalgia at her dreams, but she dismisses them – with a sigh – as childish fantasies and resumes her vacuum cleaning. (Bernard, 1971: 156)

This poem explores precisely how the deeply divided woman

can live the role culturally assigned to her by the institution of marriage only through denial and avoidance, adaptive defensive processes that can lock women into accepting self-sacrificial dependencies. In the end, despite being disturbed by a restless striving for something she is not aware that she has lost, the wife reaches a 'kind of reconciliation that is easy to interpret as happiness'.

Reticence and rape: the testimony of the poet

I want to mention one more poem from Rich's early poetry (prior to 1955), because it seems to anticipate Rich's later concern with male (sexual) violence as well as her questioning of patriarchal religious forms. 'The Perennial Answer' – which was written while Rich was an undergraduate around 1950–51, though not collected till 1955 – was probably influenced by Robert Frost's poems about rural women (*CEP*: 103).[2] This poem explores the dichotomy between the pure wife and the defiled whore of Judaeo-Christian thought, which even today among certain groups would have the power to condemn the woman who seeks outside of marriage 'for warmth'. In this narrative poem, marriage is depicted as 'a room so strange and lonely' that the girl-bride asks 'How could I help but look beyond that wall / And probe the lawful stones that built it strong / With questions sharper than a pitchfork's prong?' She is bound to 'A man not made for love, / But built for things of violence', who, enraged with possessive jealousy, rapes her:

> No matter if my tale was false or true,
> I was a woodcut figure on the page,
> On trial for a nameless sin. Then rage
> Took him like fire where lightning dives, I knew
> That he could kill me then, but what he did
> Was wrench me up the stairs, onto the bed.

The woman is prejudged guilty, an eternal Eve on trial for a 'nameless sin', and the man, violent with suspicion, turns to rape as his solution to the problem. Rich is here beginning to explore what Susan Brownmiller was later to term 'the real life deployment of the penis as a weapon . . . It is nothing more or less than a conscious process of intimidation by which *all men* keep *all women* in a state of fear (Brownmiller, 1976: 1, 5). Though in the reticent fifties the woman avoids spelling out what happened to her, she is nonetheless talking about rape within marriage. However, following the husband's death, the woman speaks out, a victim no more, and contemplates her freedom: 'at last I was alone / In an existence finally my own.' At no point is the sexual history or the character of the woman cross-examined, nor is her 'testimony' questioned: no blame can or should be attached to the woman, for the violence done to her. These recognitions – not spelt out, not politically focused – will doubtless fuel the radical feminism to come.

Woman and mother and poet: splits within the self

Rich was troubled by the split between herself as poet and herself as woman and then, more deeply, as wife. But the split between her *self* as poet/writer and her *self* as mother went deepest of all. Rich tells us that 'I plunged in my early twenties into marriage and had three children before I was thirty' (*LSS*: 42). An eight-year gap separates the second volume of poetry from the third: difficult, intensely ambivalent years in which Rich alternated between 'longing to be free' of responsibility, and being 'tied by every fibre of one's being' to her three boys, David, Paul and Jacob (*OWB*: 22). Rich's anger, guilt, weariness and demoralisation, as well as her tenderness and love, for her children, is extensively documented in *Of Woman Born*. At times, because she expressed her own needs so violently, she tells us that she felt herself to be an unnatural mother: 'I was Kali, Medea, the sow that devours her own farrow, the unwomanly woman in flight from womanhood, a Nietzschean monster' (*OWB*: 32). As a mother, Rich swung from experiencing 'blissful gratification and tenderness' to feeling bitterly resentful, depressed, angry, trapped and physically exhausted (ibid.: 21). At times, she became overwhelmed by a sense of powerlessness and felt agonisingly out of contact with the wellsprings of her writing: 'I remember thinking I would never dream again (the unconscious of the young mother – where does it entrust its messages, when dream-sleep is denied her for years?)' (ibid.: 32).

Tillie Olsen's poignant lament, 'Silences', in a talk given at Radcliffe in 1962, speaks of the troubled experience of mother-hood and writing: 'motherhood means being instantly interruptable, responsive, responsible. . . . It is distraction, not meditation, that becomes habitual; interruption, not continuity; spasmodic, not constant toil. . . . Work interrupted, deferred, relin-quished, makes blockage – at best, lesser accomplishment. Unused capacities atrophy, cease to be' (Olsen, 1980: 18–19). Only the self-discipline of desperation – and becoming harder and harder on herself – allowed Rich to survive as a writer:

August 1965, 3.30 A.M.

Necessity for a more unyielding discipline of my life.
Recognise the uselessness of blind anger.
Limit society.
Use children's school hours better, for work and solitude.
Refuse to be distracted from own style of life.
Less waste.
Be harder and harder on poems. (*OWB*: 31)

Loneliness and isolation add to the frustrations of this period in Rich's life, in which the only contact with like-minded women came through books.

Looking back to the fifties, Rich remembers 'sitting, house-bound with three young children, and with a great rage inside me, reading Wollstonecraft, Margaret Fuller, Olive Schreiner, George Eliot, and, at last, Simone de Beauvoir, my growing consciousness fragmentary and unshared and with no place to go' (Rich, 1976b: 123). Rich would never have called herself a feminist at this point: 'it was only reading *The Second Sex* that gave me the courage to write "Snapshots"' (Bulkin, 1977: 50). This poem identifies itself as 'female', and breaks out of the oppressive expectations – of the male-dominated publishing houses, literary critics, academic estab-lishments and the rest – that poetry should be 'universal', and should not speak about private, individual distress, still less about the personal difficulties of being a housewife, mother, daughter, sister or woman poet.

Woman as Other: political roots in liberal feminism

Simone de Beauvoir's inspirational existentialist insights in *The Second Sex*, which was first published in English in 1953, were an invaluable resource for Rich (De Beauvoir, 1953: 171). De Beauvoir's book is one of the most thoroughly researched articulations of liberal feminism and it sees women's commitment to femininity as limiting the development of their full human potential: the feminine woman may be beautiful, decorative and charming but is also passive, weak, deferential, and acts as a mere adjunct to the male. Women's oppression in liberal feminism is seen as the limitation, inhibition and distortion of women's human potential by a society that is dominated by men. Women's liberation is to be achieved through the attempt to free women from the confines of femininity, which society has traditionally viewed as women's biological, essential nature. In the poem, the feminine woman whose existence is bound up with being as beautiful as men desire her to be, is called into question. The ornamental 'she' of 'Snapshots of a Daughter-in-Law', having 'only the song / of silk against her knees / and these adjusted in the reflections of an eye', or she who 'shaves her legs until they gleam / like petrified mammoth-tusk' in order to be pleasing to men, is represented as either sad, or ridiculous (*CEP*: 145–9). In a liberal feminist analysis, their manipulations would be considered to be unfortunate survival tactics used by those compelled to live through another.

De Beauvoir's analysis of woman as Other allowed Rich to recognise that her own situation of distress was not unique, that this was a political rather than a personal phenomenon. As De Beauvoir points out:

> History has shown us that men have always kept in their hands all concrete powers; since the earliest days of the patriarchate they have thought best to keep woman in a state of dependence; their codes of law have been set up against her; and thus she has been definitely established as the Other. (1953: 171)

This analysis of woman as Other to the male as subject focused Rich's attention specifically on the power relationships between the sexes. Increasingly, in her work she will examine the concrete situations of domination and subordination in which women and men find themselves. De Beauvoir's words also legitimise the need for a woman to be present in and for her self within the relationship: 'There can be no presence of an other unless the other is also present in and for himself: which is to say that true alterity – otherness – is that of a consciousness separate from mine and substantially identical with mine' (ibid.).

Thus, in 'Snapshots', Rich tentatively and with trepidation takes up a liberal feminist stance. She strives to confront the myths of femininity and works towards establishing a 'separate' consciousness for herself as writer. That is, she strives to think differently from men, to think in female terms, about female issues and begins the process that will lead her towards the gynocentric feminism of the early seventies. It is a process of detaching her Self from conventional expectations, of evaluating her own critical reception as well as recognising the necessity to examine the legacy of the past.

The feminist inheritance in the late fifties was marginalised almost to invisibility and her poem 'Snapshots of a Daughter-in-Law' represents an initial recovery of that tradition. Rich looks back to connect with what had gone before, and seeks to make it re-available to her readers. She looks back critically to the not quite silenced women of history, as of mythology, invoking the furies, Boadicea, Emily Dickinson, and, more indirectly, Wollstonecraft and De Beauvoir. It is a long, highly allusive poem, which took two years to write, from 1958 to 1960. The poem 'was jotted in fragments during children's naps, brief hours in a library, or at 3.00AM after rising with a wakeful child' (*LSS*: 44). The struggle to be a writer against the relentless demands of domesticity is picked up in the poem:

> Reading while waiting
> for the iron to heat,
> writing, *My Life had stood – a Loaded Gun –*
> in that Amherst pantry while the jellies boil and scum,
> or, more often,
> iron-eyed and beaked and purposed as a bird,
> dusting everything on the whatnot every day of life. (*CEP*: 146)

In the poem Rich, like Virginia Woolf before her, does not seek to charm, conciliate, flatter, deceive or lie to succeed as a writer, and takes the risk of speaking from her own angry passion. Subversive angels – perhaps inkstained avatars of Virginia Woolf's now dead Angel in the House – tell her *'Have no patience'*, *'Be insatiable'*, *'Save yourself; others you cannot save'*. These whispers from the unconscious speak to her as it were from beyond death, the death also of the writer's spirit: 'They are probably angels, / since nothing hurts her any more, except / each morning's grit blowing into her eyes', for she cannot act on the voices she hears. Rich says, of the woman in the poem, that she 'thinks she is going mad; she is haunted by voices telling her to resist and rebel, voices which she can hear but not obey' (*LSS*: 45). Surveying 'Snapshots' of two generations of women, daughter and mother-in-law, Rich explores the division between the women, recognises their likeness and difference from each other. In doing so, she demonstrates the chasm between the women's actuality and their potential. Both of these women are caught within the same crushing system, the mother 'crumbling to pieces', the daughter critical of her, yet having no answers. The daughter, in her anguish, turns her rage against herself, punishes herself: 'she's let the tapstream scald her arm, / a match burn to her thumbnail, / or held her hand above the kettle's snout / right in the woolly steam' – a desperate self-mutilating act. The women take their frustration out on each other: 'all the old knives / that have rusted in my back, I drive in yours, / *ma semblable, ma soeur!*' But the poem does not leave it there.

Turning her attention to images of women from mythology, Rich notes that the much-celebrated woman of genius (Corinna), recites 'neither words nor music' that are her own. Then turning to an actual woman in history whose genius was sneered at and her words devalued, she points to the fact that Wollstonecraft herself was 'labelled harpy, shrew and whore', as a punishment for speaking her mind. Rich alludes obliquely to Wollstonecraft's famous image of woman 'in cages like the feathered race' – and, in a sense, is asking her monster/beaked bird/woman 'Poised, trembling and unsatisfied, before / an unlocked door, that cage of cages . . .' are you ready to take flight? Or will you stay dreaming of 'all that we might have been' (Wollstonecraft, 1975: 146).

'When We Dead Awaken': contributing to feminist literary criticism

The critical 'act of looking back' enacted in this poem anticipates Rich's later formulation in 'When We Dead Awaken: Writing as Re-Vision'. Recall again this much quoted passage which has proven to be foundational to feminist critical theory:

> Re-vision – the act of looking back, of seeing with fresh eyes, of entering an old text from a new critical direction – is for women more than a chapter in cultural history: it is an act of survival. Until we can understand the assumptions in which we are drenched we cannot know ourselves. And this drive to self-knowledge, for women, is more than a search for identity: it is part of our refusal of the self-destructiveness of male-dominated society. (*LSS*: 35)

On silencing: internal censorship, and the 'spectre of male judgement'

Ten years were to pass from the writing of 'Snapshots' before this template for a feminist critical approach to literature could be articulated so clearly, but the 'act of survival' encoded in the poem calls for women to become conscious of what they are living through, to awaken to themselves. Women must become critically conscious of the unhelpful assumptions circulating in cultural forms and, just as important, women must become self-consciously aware of the assumptions that inform their own choices – in order to survive within a patriarchal system. Before this can be achieved, however, there is 'a difficult and dangerous walking on the ice, as we try to find language and images for a consciousness we are just coming into, and with little in the past to support us' (*LSS*: 35).

Urging women writers to question their history of being 'Time's precious chronic invalid' – of being satisfied to 'glitter in fragments and rough drafts' – Rich calls for a radical re-examination of the situation in this stern injunction to

Sigh no more, ladies.
                              Time is male
and in his cups drinks to the fair.

Bemused by gallantry, we hear
our mediocrities over-praised,
indolence read as abnegation,
slattern thought styled intuition,
every lapse forgiven, our crime
only to cast too bold a shadow
or smash the mould straight off.

For that, solitary confinement,
tear gas, attrition shelling.
Few applicants for that honor. (*CEP*: 148)

Rich certainly walked on ice and had little support when she received very sharp reprimands from the critics following the publication of 'Snapshots' – 'I was seen as "bitter" and "personal" and to be personal was to be disqualified, and that was very shaking to me because I'd really gone out on a limb in that poem. . . . I realised I'd gotten slapped over the wrists and I didn't attempt that kind of thing for a long time again' (Bulkin, 1977: 50). There follow some three years of near-suicidal conflict: should she write what was expected – impersonal poetry, 'universal' themes, presenting herself as the dutiful daughter of the patriarchy – should she appease the critical establishment, and in the process abandon her integrity? Or be left in the cold by reviewers just as she was beginning to be able to write again? How hard it would have been at this point to decide to let go of her chance of resuming a successful career as writer/poet in the mainstream of American literary life? There were few indications then of any alternatives on offer. But, as Tillie Olsen spells out:

> These pressures toward censorship, self censorship; toward accepting, abiding by entrenched attitudes, thus falsifying one's own reality, range, vision, truth, voice are extreme for women writers. . . . Not to be able to come to one's truth or not to use it in one's writing, even in telling the truth having to 'tell it slant', robs one of drive, of conviction; limits potential stature; results in loss to literature and the comprehensions we seek in it. (Olsen, 1980: 44)

Rich, as a white middle-class woman, was in a sense privileged: she did ultimately find sufficient ego-strength to enable her to survive hostile reviews, and even though she had a struggle to maintain her writing through the demands of motherhood, she found the determination to press on. Nonetheless this positive out-come may at times have felt far from certain. These few lines are from 'The Corpse-Plant', written in 1963, the year 'Snapshots' was published:

Only death's insect whiteness
crooks its neck in a tumbler
where I placed its sign by choice (*CEP*: 209)

To censor one's writing, to abide by conventional attitudes, to silence one's self in an effort to be calm, detached, charming – in order to protect the writing from critical attack, the 'specter' of male judgement – constitutes another kind of death, the death of integrity in the writing. Intuitively resonating with the troubled writing of Virginia Woolf, Rich notes that she too was very con-scious of being overheard by men, and recognises that for her, likewise, there are 'problems of contact with herself, problems of language and style, problems of energy and survival' (*LSS*: 37).[3] Rich's essay 'When We Dead Awaken: Writing as Re-Vision' (1971/1976) emerges out of this complex and disorienting web of conflicts. Quoting from Ibsen's play *When We Dead Awake* about 'a woman's slow struggling awakening to the use to which her life has been put', Rich here offers to other women – to readers of her work – her own, hard-won, waking-from-death recognitions, pass-ing on her insights to a new generation, and reminding us: 'what *is* changing is the availability of knowledge, of vital texts, the visible effects on women's lives of seeing, hearing our wordless or negated experience affirmed and pursued further in language' (ibid.: 34).

Notes

1 Quotation from 'Poetry and Experience: Statement at a Poetry Reading', 1964 (*ARP*: 165).

2 Rich commented on reading my script that 'This poem was probably influenced by my reading of some of Frost's poems about rural women, especially "A Servant to Servants" and "The Hill-wife."'

3 For a further discussion of these issues see Part II, 'Constructing Myths of the Self', in Yorke (1991).

2 Reversing the Going Logic

How Hear the Woman 'To Her Own Speech'?

> I knew I had been experiencing something I had never experienced before. A complete reversal of the going logic in which someone speaks precisely so that more accurate hearing may take place. This woman was saying, and I had experienced, a depth hearing that takes place before the speaking – a hearing that is far more than acute listening. A hearing engaged in by the whole body that evokes speech – a new speech – a new creation. The woman had been heard to her own speech.
>
> Nelle Morton (1977: 4)

> The unconscious wants truth, as the body does. The complexity and fecundity of dreams come from the complexity and fecundity of the unconscious struggling to fulfil that desire. The complexity and fecundity of poetry come from the same struggle.
>
> Adrienne Rich (*LSS*: 188)

Reading the poems of 1965–69, collected in *Leaflets* (1969), it is plain that they enact another kind of coming to consciousness, 'A new / era is coming in. / Gauche as we are, it seems / we have to play our part' (*CEP*: 291). It is an era in which Rich becomes more and more the political activist, and becomes increasingly aware of the violence she was beginning to interpret as institutionalised within patriarchal forms. This chapter tracks the poetry through these years – with its injunction to see the social/public/political world as inter-implicated with the private/personal/intimate privacy of the home. Activist women move into the public fields of politics and protest even as they decide that their hitherto private, unrepresented lives are worthy of public and political protest. The poems begin to engage with the huge questions of sexual difference: why is it that men think, feel and behave as ruthlessly as they do? A male-defined language begins to be identified as at the root of the problem of male subjectivity. The first articulations of a theory of patriarchy appear and, to counter male dominance, women's experience is seen as providing the material ground for political organisation. The refusal to limit political perspectives to those produced within a male-defined culture brings a new focus on women's bodily specificity: women's lives and experiences are different to men's, and so women's specific, body-based experiential-perceptual fields will also be different. Identifying the specificities of living in a female body becomes crucial to formulating a politics of women's oppression. The task becomes one of 'hearing' women into speech; of returning to the writings of women in history to explore their 'truths'; and thus uncovering the 'untruths', the 'lies' lived by women in this patriarchal society.

Rich's political vision is honed by the experience of protest

During this period the Civil Rights movement, the Peace movement, the mass protests against the Vietnam War, the assassinations of Malcolm X, Martin Luther King and Robert Kennedy; and the Columbia University Strike meant that outspoken voices of social unrest were everywhere in evidence. Newspapers, the broadcast media, literature and poetry brought before the public images of the widespread social unrest. Also in the public domain were images of the – often brutal – establishment repression of dissent. The New Left was making strong revolutionary demands for an end to racism, violence, war, pollution of natural resources, poverty, and educational inequality.

The year 1968 saw Rich moving to New York with her family, and appointed to teach in the SEEK Program at City College. She had decided to work with 'disadvantaged' students and wished to involve herself with 'the real life of the city', a city then riven by strikes, turbulence, disruption, poverty, civil conflict, a 'city where parents were demanding community control of the schools', and where white Western supremacism was immediately and radically being questioned (*LSS*: 53, 55; *WIFT*: 24). Her assigned task at City College was simply to 'turn the students on' to writing, but this is something of an understatement in such a volatile situation. Using texts drawn from the map of her own reading as well as those she felt would enable students to discover 'the validity and variety of their own experience', Rich ranges from 'D.H. Lawrence, W.E.B. DuBois, LeRoi Jones, Plato, Orwell, Ibsen, poets from W.C. Williams to Audre Lorde' (*LSS*: 57, 56). The late sixties witnessed an upsurge of Black writing of all kinds – leaflets, pamphlets, poetry, prose, politics, polemic – and Rich found her white liberal assumptions shaken by these very powerful voices now emerging from a previously submerged culture. She had read Jean-Paul Sartre, Albert Camus and Albert Memmi, who wrote on colonialism in the fifties. Now, though continuing to read from a wide range of radical texts, she was to learn as much from her students as from her ongoing reading of the Black classics. These included W.E.B. DuBois on race, Frederick Douglass on slavery, Franz Fanon, Malcolm X and his published speeches, James Baldwin, Larry Neal (who was a colleague at City College), and the writings of her students. Chekhov's *Sakhalin Journals*, Barbara Deming's *Prison Notes*, and the writings of the New Left were also important. Through her teaching work in the SEEK Program, Rich adds further dimensions to an already comprehensive knowledge of radical thought and comes to see 'Politics as expression of the impulse to create, an expanded sense of what's "humanly possible" – this, in the late 1960s and the early women's movement, was what we tasted, not just the necessities of reactive organising and fighting back' (*WIFT*: 25; Rich quotes from Rosa Luxemburg).

In the thick of the political ferment of these years, through intellectual ideas and public activism, as well as through this dynamic experience of teaching basic writing, Rich was to recognise that it is possible to create and use a language in and through which to break out of silence. Language may be used to bear witness for oneself and one's people, to disidentify with the dominant culture, to describe and analyse, to validate, to set free from imposed dictates, rather than accept a predetermined version of what is. Rich learned first hand that 'language is power': increasingly she recognised the revolutionary potential of language to change reality for those 'suffering from injustice':

> as Simone Weil says, those who suffer from injustice most are the least able to articulate their suffering; and that the silent majority, if released into language, would not be content with a perpetuation of the conditions which have betrayed them. But this notion hangs on a special conception of what it means to be released into language: not simply learning the jargon of an elite, fitting unexceptionably into the status quo, but learning that language can be used as a means of changing reality. (*LSS*: 67)

In the terms of the writers then influencing the New Left (Marcuse, Althusser, Wilhelm Reich, Norman O. Brown), what this experience highlighted was that the logic of domination controlling the universe of discourse could be challenged, and what was needed was a heightened awareness of the role of language. If language can limit, direct and control responses, structure reality, structure consciousness, define and confine the self, then it may also enable us to formulate thought, to interpret and analyse issues, to reflect, to criticise, to rename, to recreate. In short, if language can be a means to change reality, then language can become a powerful weapon in the war against oppression.

This period is marked by increasing activism and specifically by a greater involvement of women (and women poets) in a variety of public issues. We find Rich bearing political witness in reconstructing the protest of 36-year-old Russian poet and activist Natalia Gorbanevskaya who, in sitting down on the parapet of Lofno Mesto, the old execution platform in Red Square, participates in a demonstration against the Soviet invasion of Czechoslovakia:

> ... At noon we sit down quietly on the parapet
> and unfurl our banners
> almost immediately
> the sound of police whistles

from all corners of Red Square
                          we sit
quietly and offer no resistance
Is this your little boy

we will relive this over and over

the banners torn from our hands
                    blood flowing
a great jagged torn place
in the silence of complicity (*CEP*: 300)

A letter, written by Natalia Gorbanevskaya, was smuggled out
and published in the *New York Times* just before her arrest. The
repressiveness of the totalitarian Russian State, as repressive as the
West in this Cold War period, can be seen in the committal of
Gorbanevskaya by a Moscow court to confinement for three years
in a 'special' psychiatric hospital in Kazan – operated by secret
police.[1] The poem, dated August 1968, is fascinating, poised as it is
at a moment when women are just beginning to recognise the political need to 'pool that intelligence, that experience, that tactical
and strategic ability at present fragmented into separate struggles'
and to identify women's own issues as worthy of political protest
(Firestone, 1979: 3). In the poem, Rich crucially identifies as significant and worthy of notice this mother/poet's protest despite
what at the time seemed to be 'a most trivial event' involving six or
seven men and women 'unfurling a few home-made signs and one
home-made Czech flag', protesting against the Soviet invasion of
Czechoslovakia (Gorbanevskaya, 1972: 9). It lasted only a few min-
utes: 'only a few score people witnessed it before plainclothes
Soviet security agents roughed up the demonstrators and rushed
them out of the square in commandeered cars'. Importantly, however, women are shown as no longer to be identified with the
'silence of complicity'. The poem marks a major shift in Rich's
thought. The 'new era' of heightened woman-awareness identified
in 'The Demon Lover' is beginning to become politicised in the dis-
tinctly feminist terms of woman-identified specificity: 'The woman
who has spent time in a hospital fearing to lose the child in her
body, the woman who has suffered the judgement of her sanity by
a jury of male experts, knows something of Gorbanevskaya's
ordeal' (*LSS*: 119). Rich clearly identifies her specific vulnerability

as a pregnant woman – she shows just how easily an activist woman can become labelled as mentally unstable: psychiatric incarceration is one very effective method of political pacification in ruthless male-dominated societies, East or West. These unacceptable modes of restraint are to be identified as 'methods specifically available against women in male-dominated society' (*LSS*: 118).

Nearer to home, those opposed to the US war in Vietnam demonstrated against the appalling atrocities committed by US soldiers: the torture, rape and slaughter of women; the napalm, white phosphorus, fragmentation bombs used deliberately on a civilian population; the poisoning of crops, defoliation of forests and indiscriminate maiming of children. Vietnam was at the forefront of media attention and no one could avoid the nightmare of war. For the woman poet there is a struggle to understand, to grasp this ruthless mindset, to understand how it was that ordinary, average Americans were able to do what they did in the war – but incomprehension begins to slide into condemnation of 'the enemy', envisioned here as 'the prince of air and darkness'. What was the answer? Rich spells out her thoughts in 'The Phenomenology of Anger': the dream or fantasy she has is of burning away his lies and of leaving him in a new world:

When I dream of meeting
the enemy, this is my dream:

white acetylene
ripples from my body
effortlessly released
perfectly trained
on the true enemy

raking his body down to the thread
of existence
burning away his lie
leaving him in a new
world; a changed
man (*FDF*: 166)

Many critics were disturbed by this imagery which they saw as man-hating. But the lines need to be read carefully and placed in the context of Rich's thought in *On Lies, Secrets, and Silence*. When she speaks of 'the enemy' – 'the prince of air and darkness' – she creates a mythic figure symbolising the forces of destructive domination, which she hates. It is his 'lie', his 'words', and his 'mask' of utter indifference that are symbolically 'burned' away by the acetylene burner. Rich uses her dream/poem to voice her urgent longing for 'truth': 'I tell you, truth is, at the moment, here / burning outward through our skins' (*FDF*: 106). Her critique clearly relates to the *language* used by the dominating forces, and the apparent male inability to feel:

I hate the mask you wear . . .
I hate your words
they make me think of fake
revolutionary bills
crisp imitation parchment
they sell at battlefields.

Last night, in this room, weeping
I asked you: *what are you feeling?*
do you feel anything? (*FDF*: 167)

The woman's 'hate', rather than being directed to men as such, is thus directed towards the words and actions of those male-dominated governments, institutions, agencies who inculcated and perpetuated the violence, who were ultimately responsible for atrocities committed during the war. The individual numbed-out soldier 'gunning down the babies at My Lai' and 'burning the crops / with some new sublimate' is, nonetheless, the same man who shares the bed. How can this be? The poet struggles with this, and images his turning away from feeling as a twisting of the body: she senses it 'in the torsion of your body / as you defoliate the fields we lived from'. At the same time, she cherishes a dream that things might have been different: 'I would have loved to live in a world / of women and men gaily / in collusion with green leaves, stalks, / building mineral cities, transparent domes, / little huts of woven grass / each with its own pattern . . .' Fundamentally, restoring the connection to feeling is at the root of her politics at this time. As she wrote in a journal in 1969:

The moment when a feeling enters the body – is political. This touch is political. By which I mean, that *politics* is the effort to find ways of humanely dealing with each other – as groups or as individuals – politics being simply process, the breaking down of barriers of oppression, tradition, culture, ignorance, fear, self-protectiveness. (*WIFT*: 24)

Rich's poem 'Tear Gas' is dated 12 October 1969, and is also located very much at the turning point when feminist thought is grappling with the idea that the violence and ruthlessness of the power of patriarchy as a system permeate everything, 'even the language in which we describe it' (*FDF*: 198–200, *OWB*: 58). At a protest against the treatment of GI prisoners, when demonstrators were tear-gassed, the poet explores the fearful experience of being a woman and of 'stepping into the male field / of violence' (*FDF*: 198). The poem highlights Rich's disillusion with the New Left's revolutionary promises: their vision is too narrow, their political premises are too theoretical, too abstracted from experience. The poet wants change, but not, as she saw it then, in the male-defined terms of Marxist revolution:

> It wasn't completeness I wanted
> (the old ideas of a revolution that could be foretold, and once
>   arrived at would give us ourselves and each other)
> I stopped listening long ago to their descriptions
> of the good society
>
> The will to change begins in the body not in the mind
> My politics is in my body, accruing and expanding with every
>   act of resistance and each of my failures
> Locked in the closet at 4 years old I beat the wall with my body
> that act is in me still (*FDF*: 199)

Identifying the impulse to politics and protest as emerging from a kind of unconscious knowing within the body, Rich anticipates here a basic premise of her thought: that as women we need to listen within to the language of the body which holds our deepest understandings. Indeed, our lives depend on such ways of knowing: 'our skin is alive with signals; our lives and our deaths are inseparable from the release or blockage of our thinking bodies' (*OWB*: 284). These lines also underscore the imperative concerns voiced later in *Of Woman Born*, that 'the repossession by women of our bodies will bring far more essential change to human society than the seizing of the means of production by workers' (*OWB*: 285).

This crucial statement marks her radical feminist break away from the politics of the New Left, though through the eighties – in the context of an acceleration of corporate power during the years of the Reagan/Thatcher administrations, the Sandinista revolution and the politics of Central American Solidarity – Rich was to reassess her relation to Marx: 'I sit down and pick up a second-hand, faintly annotated student copy of Marx's *The German Ideology*, which "happens" to be lying on the table' (*BBP*: 211). Raya Dunayevskaya's book, *Women's Liberation and the Dialectics of Revolution*, was also extremely important. Reading widely, particularly the work of West Indian Marxists, C.L.R. James and Eric Williams, restored her to connection with the philosophic and organisational struggles of the radical movements of the Left. In re-visioning this connection, she will highlight once more the diverse threads which continued to be woven in and through her work overall, of her earlier commitment to the various movements for liberation that were active during the sixties.

Identifying the body as a source of insight and language

The 'body', in Rich's thought during the late sixties, seems to be the source of signals which have the potential to enable a woman to reach beneath patriarchal language for another kind of knowing: 'I am really asking whether women cannot begin, at last, to *think through the body*' (*OWB*: 284). Is she suggesting that the woman's body itself may 'speak', offering its subtle messages to consciousness as another available mode of cognitive potentiality? The poet is engaged in a struggle to create a language emerging from her (female) body, that will not only reach out to others, but will also allow her as a woman a means to release her self into language:

> I needed to touch you
> with a hand, a body
> but also with words
> I need a language to hear myself with
> to see myself in
> a language like pigment released on the board

blood-black, sexual green, reds
veined with contradictions
bursting under pressure from the tube (*FDF*: 199)

The language needed by the poet/woman must allow the contradictory, previously censored, unconscious mind/body to be
explosively released from repression, emerging into consciousness as 'blood-black, sexual green, reds / veined with
contradictions'. Surely these vibrant primary colours signal the
poet's desire for the visibility and body-integrity of a woman-made
language in which she can identify her self, not as the 'Other', i.e.
as the recipient of and subject to the projections, internalisations,
predictions, presumptions of a phallocentric denial of female presence, but rather as tuning in to her own, bodily based and
experiential perceptual fields, engaged, that is, in the revelatory
task of discovery of her own desiring presence to her self? The
search for a language that will adequately articulate women's experience has begun.

Women's revolution: undoing the structures of male domination

Radical feminism begins around this time to construct a new political and social theory of women's oppression. Kate Millett's now
classic work, *Sexual Politics*, appears in 1970, and in that book she
takes on the task of theorising 'patriarchy'. She argues that our
society 'like all other historical civilisations is a patriarchy . . . if one
recalls that the military, industry, technology, universities, science,
political office, and finance – in short, every avenue of power within
the society, including the coercive force of the police, is entirely in
male hands' (Millett, 1977: 25). The fundamental challenge in
Millett's eyes is to undo the power structures of male domination
within patriarchal forms. Women's liberation demands a feminist
cultural revolution involving re-education and political and economic reorganisation rather than organising 'through the theatrics
of armed struggle' (ibid.: 363). The sexual revolution required a
transformation in consciousness – 'the exposure and elimination of
social and psychological realities underlining political and cultural

structures' – and this would produce the most meaningful changes within society, as well as in the quality of life (ibid.: 362). Some women active in politics felt powerfully this imperative to reorganise politically. Many women who had channelled their energy into other dissenting movements, the Civil Rights Movement, for example, decided at this time to put their energy into women's issues. At a 'Congress to Unite Women', which was convened during 1969, Koedt et al. declared that:

> the uniqueness of our revolution transcends economic, racial, generational, and political differences, and that these differences must be transcended in action, the common interest of our liberation, self-determination and development of our political movement. (Koedt et al., 1973: 309)

Radical feminism begins to theorise sexism as the root oppression: women as a social group are oppressed by men as a social group, and that is the primary oppression which crosses race and culture as well as class boundaries. Patriarchy, which is almost universal, is the oppressing structure of male domination. As a theory, radical feminism is created by and for women, and upholds as a principle woman-centredness. It focuses on women's lived experience and interests, produces analyses of male power and structures of male dominance from women's perspectives, and theorises, with more and more complexity, male violence against women, seen from women's points of view. By the mid-seventies the control of and violence done to women's bodies becomes a central focus of radical feminist thought.

'Caryatid: Two Columns', published in 1973, contains Rich's major statements about the Vietnam experience. Feminist anger and a collective sense of political engagement in a cultural revolution fuse explosively in these 'columns', which release Rich's justified feminist fury into print. She comes to the conclusion that 'the bombings are so wholly sadistic, gratuitous and demonic that they can finally be seen, if we care to see them, for what they are: acts of concrete sexual violence, an expression of the congruence of violence and sex in the masculine psyche' (*LSS*: 109). Manhood – 'potency – with the objectification of another's person and the domination of another's body' comes under fire itself as a 'venereal disease that lives alike in the crimes of Vietnam and the lies of sexual liberation . . . as it lives in the imaginations of pornographers, in the fantasies of poets and presidents, professors and policemen, surgeons and salesmen' (*LSS*: 110).

Masculinity and male bonding – what Heidi Hartman will later identify as those 'relations between men, which have a material base, and which, though hierarchical, establish or create interdependence and solidarity among men that allow them to dominate women' – are both clearly recognised as problematic (Hartman, 1981: 14). Deeply identified with the misuse of power, macho-masculinity involves a profound dissociation of sensibility and this, coupled with the tendency to dehumanise the Other, allows the violent atrocities perpetrated by men – whether against other men, against women, or against children – to continue unabated.

In disidentifying herself from the New Left, and in seeing their activities as dominated intellectually by men having too narrow a vision, Rich also sees leftist women as

> no more in a position to demasculinize the nature of society than women of any other political persuasion. At present a stronger unconscious, psychic alliance exists between the men of the worldwide Left and the men ruling the most powerful patriarchy in history, than between the men of the Left and the feminist movement. (*LSS*: 116)

Taking Kate Millett's analysis further in *Of Woman Born*, Rich argued that 'the cross-cultural, global domination of women by men can no longer be either denied or defended. When we acknowledge this, we tear open the relationship at the core of all power-relationships, a tangle of lust, violence, possession, fear, conscious longing, unconscious hostility, sentiment, rationalization: the sexual understructure of social and political forms' (*OWB*: 56). As we have seen, sex and violence are, in Rich's analysis, inextricably inter-implicated in the power structures of patriarchy. Rich eventually formulates her own definition of patriarchy, which she expresses in *Of Woman Born*:

> Patriarchy is the power of the fathers: a familial-social, ideological, political system in which men – by force, direct pressure, or through ritual, tradition, law, and language, customs, etiquette, education, and the division of labor, determine what part women shall or shall not play, and in

which the female is everywhere subsumed under the male . . . The power of the fathers has been difficult to grasp because it permeates everything, even the language in which we try to describe it. (*OWB*: 57–8)

Rich has clearly moved on from the liberal feminist voice which could be heard intermittently through the fifties and the early to mid-sixties. The De Beauvoirean insights relating to woman as Other are being refined and developed further, and Rich's thought moves closer to radical feminist politics, especially in seeing the relationship between male and female as a power-structured relationship, in which females are controlled and dominated by males.

Sexual difference: male-dominated language

Also influenced by Mary Daly's *Beyond God the Father*, Rich clearly identifies sexual difference as rooted in the difference between male and female cultures, and as demonstrable in the ways in which women and men think: 'for centuries, patriarchy has maintained itself by asking what was good for males, has assumed male norms and values as universal ones, has allowed the differences of "otherness", the division of male and female consciousness, to become a terrifying dissociation of sensibility' (*LSS*: 111). Women, in Daly's view, have a very different experience to that of men and therefore speak from a different frame of reference: 'What is required of women at this point in history is a firm and deep refusal to limit our perspectives, questioning, and creativity to any of the preconceived patterns of male-dominated culture' (Daly, 1986: 7). Daly's powerful call for women to liberate 'language from its old context' in order to 'breakthrough to new semantic fields' deeply informs Rich's thought in the early seventies. The liberation of language in Daly's thought involves a cutting away of 'language and images that reflect and perpetuate the structures of a sexist world', and thus deconstructing 'the phallic value system imposed by patriarchy' (ibid.: 8, 9).

Cutting away the distorting sexist 'dreams' of a man 'asleep in the next room' is very much the theme of 'Incipience', a poem written in 1971 (*FDF*: 155–7). The women of this poem enact the 'dissection' of male-defined language and images from a man's brain in order to step 'outside the frame of his dream':

> A man is asleep in the next room
>> We are his dreams
>> We have the heads and breasts of women
>> the bodies of birds of prey
>> Sometimes we turn into silver serpents
> While we sit up smoking and talking of how to live
> he turns on the bed and murmurs
>
> A man is asleep in the next room
>> A neurosurgeon enters his dream
>> and begins to dissect his brain
>> She does not look like a nurse
>> she is absorbed in her work
>> she has a stern, delicate face like Marie Curie
> She is not / might be either of us
>
> A man is asleep in the next room
>> He has spent a whole day
>> standing, throwing stones into the black pool
>> which keeps its blackness
>
> Outside the frame of his dream we are stumbling up the hill
>> hand in hand, stumbling and guiding each other
>> over the scarred volcanic rock

The task of this poem is to find symbolic ways to disrupt the power and potency of limiting male-defined words and intrapsychic images in order to release women (and men?) from bondage to the preconceptions of phallocentrism – it involves most profoundly 'the dislodging of images that reflect and reinforce the prevailing social arrangements' (Daly, 1986: 10). Thus, in her developing analysis through the late sixties and early seventies, Rich was to develop her sense of the difference in mentality between men and women as perceivable in the language used by women as compared to men: she critically analyses the spoken words, as well as identifying gender differences in that which was compelled to remain secret, silenced, unspoken within cultural forms. It becomes increasingly difficult for politically aware women to remain within the 'silence of complicity' (*FDF*: 89). Male thought, male subjectivity, male language, the posturings of macho-masculinity and the oppressiveness of male sexuality come under intense scrutiny and are found utterly wanting.

The big question, of course, is how do women begin to speak 'new words'? Mary Daly, in *Beyond God the Father* reflects on how this might happen:

> It would be a mistake to imagine that the new speech of women can be equated simply with women speaking men's words. What is happening is that women are really *hearing ourselves* and each other, and out of this supportive hearing emerge new words. (1986: 8)

Mary Daly was I think the first to voice this necessity. Nelle Morton, three years later, reiterated this need for women to engage in 'hearing each other into speech' (Morton, 1977). And Rich's urgent questions? She asks, 'How do we listen?' 'How do we make it possible for another to break her silence?' (*LSS*: 185). They are huge questions – for, indeed, how do we break the silences of our life and times?

These revolutionary calls for women to seize language and speak their way into a transformed subjectivity startlingly anticipate later, much more complex theorising. The poet's language here does not deny the effort or the strain of self-creation – nor does it simplify the difficulty in finding a language that can articulate *what she means* when she speaks *as a woman*. The poet is limited by having to use a language that fails her: 'this is not what I mean / these images are not what I mean'. The failure of language to express women's meaning becomes an insistent theme within the poems.

In 'Meditations for a Savage Child', a poem about a wild, feral child, the wounding and scarring of the 'wild' woman poet/Savage Child's throat becomes a metaphor for the violence done to the poet, in having to use an imposed language and forms of naming that fail to render her meanings adequately:

When I try to speak
my throat is cut
and, it seems, by his hand

The sounds I make are prehuman, radical
the telephone is always
ripped-out

and he sleeps on
Yet always the tissue
grows over, white as silk

hardly a blemish
maybe a hieroglyph for scream (*FDF*: 181)

The scarring of the body again attests to the violence embedded
in the silence. These wounds amount to a kind of torture inflicted
by an inadequate 'provided' language which fails to render or trans-
mit either the wild child's or the woman poet's way of knowing – so
that it may be known. The resulting invisibility/inaudibility of
each's experiences and values constitutes an obliteration of their
identity and voice: they are subjected to an 'intellectual coercion of
which they are not even consciously aware. In a world where language and naming are power, silence is oppression, is violence'
(*LSS*: 204). And so the poet finds an apt metaphor for that particular cruelty: a silenced voice – an identity in agony, screaming but
not heard – and the scar a visible, indecipherable mark, 'a hieroglyph for a scream'.

Mary Daly's *Beyond God the Father* inspired feminists to begin
to explore women's liberation as a 'dislodging process', in which
'the names imposed upon reality by male-dominated society' were
to be rejected as oppressive:

> Women will free traditions, thought, and customs only by hearing
> each other and thus making it possible to speak our word. This
> involves interaction between insight and praxis, not in the sense of
> 'reflection' upon 'social action' (a false dualism), but rather in the
> sense of a continual growth, flexibility, and emergence of new per-
> ceptions of reality – perceptions that come from being where one is.
> (1986: 10–11)

The presence of the other woman is absolutely crucial to this
'dislodging process'. In 'Planetarium' (1968), an astonishing visionary poem, Rich celebrates the life and work of Caroline Herschel
(1750–1848), 'astronomer, sister of William; and others', as 'she
whom the moon ruled / like us / levitating into the night
sky / riding the polished lenses' (*FDF*: 114). In this reclaiming of
a woman of history whose vision 'changed the body of knowledge
in astronomy', we find the newly perceptive Rich watching and

listening for the 'unheard voices' of her sisters, hearing them out and trying to decipher their meanings (Welchel, 1984: 56). In a strong identification with Caroline Herschel, she celebrates connectedness between women as well as identifying, through the images she uses, both the silencing and the speech – as impulses of light, radio impulses, a 'battery of signals' – from 'Galaxies of women, there' in the night sky (*FDF*: 115). For the first time we find Rich identifying her aggressive poetic creativity as female; and the monster-woman of earlier poems is no longer alone – there are now many other unwomanly women 'doing penance for impetuousness' inhabiting the skies (*RAR*: 57).

> A woman in the shape of a monster
> a monster in the shape of a woman
> the skies are full of them

These female 'stars' send impulses of 'light exploding / from the core', which bombard the poet, which 'travel through me' and which pierce her as receiver of their signals:

> ... I am an instrument in the shape
> of a woman trying to translate pulsations
> into images   for the relief of the body
> and the reconstruction of the mind. (*FDF*: 116)

Stars, in the 'companion poem', 'Orion', are related to painful facts which pierce through or penetrate the woman's body, and many images of violent piercing – whether of spears, of hail, or of nails – recur in the poems at this time, for example here, in 'The Days: Spring' (*FDF*: 79–80):[2]

> Later the stars come out like facts,
> my constellation streams at my head,
> a woman's body nailed with stars. (*CEP*: 417)

In the political transformation that radical feminism has wrought, Rich is now ready to take the dangerous step through to another way of knowing the world – a world of commitment to women – and to take up a gynocentric rather than an androcentric point of view.

Ethical integrity and the body of 'truth'

To imagine the reconstruction of the mind within a poem is one thing – but the breaking of silences, the transformation of habitual ways of thinking and interacting, and, ultimately, the creation of 'a new ethics . . . a new morality' demands a challenging scrutiny of women's collusive strategies for survival within patriarchal systems (*LSS*: 185). In the brief, yet profound and urgent 'Women and Honor: Some Notes on Lying' (1975), Rich points to the necessity for relationships between women to be closely examined. Typically she puts herself on the line: 'I wrote *Women and Honor* in an effort to make myself more honest, and to understand the terrible negative power of the lie in relationships between women'. If men may (sometimes!) have told the truth about facts, 'they have not been expected to talk about feelings at all' (*LSS*: 186). Women have traditionally talked about feelings but, in order to survive, have nonetheless developed ways of avoiding facing the more difficult truths of relationship. If women's relationships with other women are to have ethical integrity, a deeper honesty has to be upheld as a feminist value, for 'Lying is done with words, and also with silence . . .' (ibid.: 187). 'Women and Honor' seems to me to deepen our understanding of Rich's conception of the patriarchal 'lie': 'patriarchal lying has manipulated women both through falsehood and through silence. Facts we need have been withheld from us. False witness has been borne against us' – internalisation of patriarchal values has required women to be untruthful to themselves (ibid.: 189). Women's fear of being controlled by others or of losing control of themselves can lead to manipulatory survival strategies in which openness and contact with the *other* as well as with the deeper self is lost; a woman's integrity to her own truths can thereby be undermined. Amnesia – repression, denial, forgetting – is the outcome: 'amnesia is the silence of the unconscious'. The resulting loss of contact with the unconscious mind leads to a loss of connection with the body of 'truth':

> The unconscious wants truth. It ceases to speak to those who want something else more than truth.
>
> In speaking of lies, we come inevitably to the subject of truth. There is nothing simple or easy about this idea. There is no 'the truth', 'a

truth' – truth is not one thing, or even a system. It is an increasing complexity. (ibid.: 188)

Truth is no absolute in this conception: it can be contradictory, ambiguous and confusing, yet such truthfulness and *an increasing complexity* is the only honourable way for women to relate to each other. The task of describing women's experience and reality in all its complexity 'as candidly and fully as we can to each other' becomes an urgent political necessity as women strive to articulate a woman-centred vision, and this was essentially the task of consciousness-raising groups throughout the seventies (ibid.: 190). Far from being originary and absolute, such 'truth' can be seen as comparable to psychoanalytic 'truth' which is relative, unfixed, and actually neither true nor false in that it is always already *an interpretation* within language. Yet the crucial difference is that the new interpretation is woman-centred: these perceptions are organised around the specific experience of living socially as a woman, and in that they are experienced in and through a female body, they are radically different from male-centred perceptions. In basing her woman-centred political theory around the experience of women's bodies, sexuality and lives, Rich aligns herself with the structures of radical feminist thought, which has in turn stressed the urgency of organising politically around the articulation of women's experience.

Sexual difference: placing women's experience at the centre

Radical feminism has thus played its part in transforming the structures of Rich's thought. Following Mary Daly, Dale Spender, in her trenchant and much criticised book, *Man Made Language*, asserts: 'it is males who have named the world. It is probably inevitable that those who perform naming should do so from their own point of view, taking themselves as the centre, the reference point, and naming all else in relation to themselves' (1980: 54). Turning this round, as we have seen, Rich places women at the centre of her perceptual field and, in displacing phallogocentric systems of thought, begins to write *as a woman*:

To write directly and overtly as a woman, out of a woman's body and experience, to take women's existence seriously as theme and source for art, was something I had been hungering to do, needing to do, all my writing life. It placed me nakedly face to face with both terror and anger; it did indeed *imply the breakdown of the world as I had always known it, the end of safety.* (*BBP*: 182)[3]

I have tried to show how the focus on uncovering body-based experiential perceptions, a focus on 'specificity' – that is, on the concrete and particular experiences of women – has organised Rich's thought and political orientation. The next chapter identifies the maternal matrix as one such specifically female sphere, delineated by the culturally sanctioned presumptions and coercive regulatory systems of patriarchy. In her book *Of Woman Born*, Rich identifies the institution of motherhood as historically appropriated by the oppressive economies and social coercions of white Western patriarchal forms. In her focus on the body, Rich was inappropriately criticised for what her critics mistakenly saw as biological essentialism and matriarchal utopianism. She alters course, but continues to press for a healing of the dualistic thought forms of Western patriarchy, and reiterates her urgent call for women to rewrite the stories and to re-envision myth from a gynocentric perspective.

Notes

1 Interested readers may refer to Natalya Gorbanevskaya, *Red Square at Noon* (1972: 9) for further information. Rich discusses Gorbanevskaya's experiences in 'Caryatid: Two Columns' (*LSS*: 117).

2 See 'When We Dead Awaken: Writing as Re-Vision' (*LSS*: 47) for Rich's comments on this poem.

3 Rich paraphrases James Baldwin.

3 Embodied Experience

Passion and Politics in Of Woman Born

This chapter takes as its focus *Of Woman Born*, and picks up on Rich's stated aims for the book, which she articulates in 'Ten Years Later: A New Introduction':

> there are several old ideas cohabiting in the enclave of their privileged status: the superiority of European and Christian peoples; the claim of force as superior to the claims of relation; the abstract as a more developed or 'civilised' mode than the concrete and particular; the ascription of a higher intrinsic human value to men than to women. (*OWB*: ix)

I draw attention in this chapter to Rich's critique of emotionless, abstract logic; of dualism; and of life-denying systems of thought which would leave out the irrational, the intuitive, the spiritual – the body, the female, the otherness, the passion, the violence of women – which she sees as excluded, silenced, unacceptable. I explore her radical feminist focus on 'the concrete and particular' – the here and now, or there and then – experiences of women; her experimental method as exemplified in *Of Woman Born*; her critique of the forceful regulation of women's bodies within institutions of social control – and her brief and much-criticised excursion into the realms of anthropology to seek an alternative to patriarchal religious thought forms.

For those of us who are mothers, the experience of reading *Of Woman Born* for the first time can be devastating. As I once again risk dipping into this field of primary intensity, this force-field of power and danger, pain, love, sensuality, frustration, envy, creativity, I enter upon what can still be for many women a profound source of alienation, helplessness and destructiveness – as well as an exhilarating source of joy, hope, potentiality. Having adopted her child, Rachel Blau DuPlessis had this to say of *Of Woman Born*: 'Every part of that book described something I needed: the vulnerabilities and ambivalence, tidal washes as I struggled with this child and my life, the embittering fears of total inadequacy that sear down to a core and burn me out, the battle of wills and wits I hardly understood' (Blau DuPlessis, 1978: 394). In identifying her need for Rich's words, DuPlessis speaks for many of us who fail to find our reality represented in the texts made available through 'official' channels. Jane Lazarre also needed Rich's words: 'Her affirmation of the mother rage I know so well, her courageous and brutal exposure of that painful myth of maternal serenity, healed my inner wounds as I read, and fed the process of restoration of my self-respect as a mother' (Lazarre, 1976: 293).

In writing of motherhood, I too am caught up in this ambivalent complexity of recollection. How many women have felt the 'invisible violence of the institution of motherhood, the guilt, the powerless responsibility for human lives, the judgements and condemnations, the fear of her own power, the guilt, the guilt, the guilt' (*OWB*: 277). How many feel 'guilty' or 'responsible' for the outcomes of their mothering?

How do women act to change things if we (and our children) are so much the victim of patriarchal systems? Rich would argue that 'only the willingness to share private and sometimes painful experience can enable women to create a collective description of the world which will be truly ours' (*OWB*: 16). This focus on consciousness-raising as the source and ground for political organisation became a manifesto within radical feminism during the mid-seventies. Political theory, of necessity, had to be created out of women's lived experience. Holistic radical feminist theories upheld the authority of women's experience as at the centre of both theory and political practice. Questions looming about the constructed nature of experience had yet to be taken on board, but this making visible of an alternative understanding of the ways male-dominated systems operate, this bearing witness to the affective, economic, social and sexual fields within which mothers live out their existence, gave the lie to idealisation, to systems of thought which would blame the mother, and to the political innocence of the institution of motherhood.

Transforming thinking: the critique of dualism

The deliberately experimental structuring of *Of Woman Born*, in which the voice of subjective and emotional experience is given as much credence as the voice of academic research, is a 'radical departure from the usual methodological distancing devices': Rich's personal and creative poetic voice is not detached and separate from the voice of scholarship and disciplined logic, and this is, of course, part of her revolutionary strategy (Lazarre, 1976: 293). Her politically motivated desire is that 'Sexuality, politics, intelligence, power, motherhood, work, community, intimacy will develop new meanings; thinking itself will be transformed' (*OWB*: 286). To transform 'thinking' required a healing of the dualistic split between mind and body, between objective and subjective – and her characteristic, deep personal honesty required Rich to enter the 'heart of maternal darkness' to face the *violence* at her own core, to listen to and acknowledge her own 'unacceptable but undeniable anger' towards her own children, an anger that arose from her experience of being a mother in the 'family-centred, consumer-oriented, Freudian-American world of the 1950s', and to set that acknowledgement against patriarchal idealisations of motherhood (*OWB*: 24–5).

Thus Rich herself engaged in a (therapeutic? consciousness-raising? psychoanalytic?) process of 'unforgetting', in describing the realities of her own experience – and that of other mothers – as candidly and fully as she could. The individual's apparently private experience of motherhood – her own as well as that of 'the mothers around me and before me' – had been buried in the repressive silences of the period. And in this speaking we hear a shocking personal voice. It is a shocking book. Alexander Theroux, in his condemnatory review, commented sourly: it is 'less a feminist manifesto than the "Confessions of St. Adrienne." A hodgepodge of ten aggrieved essays. . . . This book is an absolute radical witchery; the bookend to its male chauvinist counterpart' (Theroux, 1976). His rage-filled outburst sees Rich in the throes of 'a kind of nervous breakdown . . . unfulfilled, guilt-ridden, depressed', and this scathing review, along with Helene Vendler's 'Myths for Mothers' which condemned *Of Woman Born* for its '"partisan writing" filled with the "rhetoric of violence"', provoked Kathleen Barry to protest against the active censorship of the book through such hostile and damaging reviews, especially by women. She helpfully reminded readers that '*Of Woman Born* was created out of a history of feminist thought and writing. It is not a one-woman statement on mothering' (Barry, 1977). But few critics realised that this mixing of 'personal testimony with research' precisely aimed to confront those complacencies which would deny, idealise, sanitise and depoliticise the personal world of mothers' experiences (*OWB*: x).

On the psychology of women: myth, madness and mothering

The themes of *Of Woman Born*, with its concern for mothers, daughters, sisters, lovers, seem to me to be prefigured in Phyllis Chesler's important 1972 indictment of psychiatric care: *Women and Madness*. Rich read Chesler in 1972 and in a 1978 footnote, though she acknowledged her work as 'groundbreaking', she was to comment: 'Chesler oversimplified . . . the mother–daughter relationship . . . she resorts to blaming the mother for the daughter's disadvantaged position in patriarchy' (*LSS*: 91). This critical engagement with Chesler's work, I would suggest, significantly informs the writing of *Of Woman Born*.

The task of Chesler's book was to examine the myths and coercions of the 'relationship between the female condition and what we call madness'. In this book 'about female psychology, or if you will, about Demeter and her four daughters, about what has happened to them in the twentieth century', Chesler draws attention to the fact that

> Female children are quite literally starved for matrimony: not for marriage, but for physical nurturance and a legacy of power and humanity from adults of their own sex ('mothers'). Most mothers prefer sons to daughters and are more physically and domestically nurturant to them. Within modern society, woman's 'dependent' and 'incestuous' personality probably stems from not being experienced as 'divine' by the mother (and father). Most women are glassed into infancy, and perhaps some forms of madness, by an unmet need for maternal nurturance. (Chesler, 1972: 18)

Specifically focused on the myths and madnesses of psychiatric assessment and care, Chesler argued that 'Clinicians, most of whom are men, all too often treat their patients, most of whom are women, as "wives" and "daughters," rather than as people: treat them as if female misery, by biological definition, exists outside the realm of what is considered human or adult' (ibid.: xxi).

Seeing women as 'impaled on the cross of self-sacrifice' and as starved of 'nurturance' not only in the physical and psychological realms of respect and compassion and care but also in the more mythological sense of '"protection", "guidance" and "intervention"', Chesler's impassioned indictment was part of an upsurge of feminist interest in female psychology, psychoanalysis and psychiatry (ibid.: 31). As Juliet Mitchell had pointed out in 1971, 'the borderline between the biological and the social which finds expression in the family is the land that psychoanalysis sets out to chart, it is the land where sexual distinction originates' (Mitchell, 1971: 167). In charting that territory, Rich herself embarked on a journey through Freud, Klein, Horney, Jung, Harding and Neumann at this time, reading intensively within the field.[1] During the exhilarating years from 1972 to 1976, the years when *Of Woman Born* was being written, the individual woman's apparently private experience of motherhood became the focus of international feminist interest, as an area of study largely unmentioned in the annals of patriarchal thought.[2] Identifying this worrying absence as evidence of a regulatory system 'which has chained us to our biology and which still keeps our bodies under male control' (Rich, 1976a), Rich points to the regulation of women's reproductive power by men in every totalitarian system and every socialist revolution, the legal and the technical control by men of contraception, fertility, abortion, obstetrics, gynaecology and extrauterine reproductive experiments – all are essential to the patriarchal system. (*OWB*: 34)

And it is this system which creates the desperation, the 'undramatic, undramatised suffering' of the private world of mothers labelled 'bad', who are scapegoated by patriarchy (ibid.: 276).

The violent underside of patriarchal mothering

Simone de Beauvoir before her had identified the frustration and discontent of the woman who was a mother and had voiced her concern for the vulnerable child: 'when it is realized how difficult woman's present situation makes her full self-realization, how many desires, rebellious feelings, just claims she nurses in secret, one is frightened at the thought that defenceless infants are abandoned to her care' (De Beauvoir, 1953: 528–9). So too Rich, in her deep compassion, refuses to collude with those who would idealise the position of the mother and leave unspoken the violent underside of the patriarchal institution of motherhood, the damage, the distress, the harm perpetrated not only by fathers, but also by some mothers on their vulnerable children. Bringing her readers face to face with the reality of maternal infanticide, she specifically highlights the situation of the mother living 'in the solitary confinement of a life at home enclosed with young children' who could, in her isolation and desperation, end up murdering her own children (*OWB*: 279). In seeing motherhood as a system in which institutions established by men regulate women's reproductive power, Rich's wide-ranging analysis offers a logic that begins to make sense of even this: the raw, undeniable evidence of mothers' violence against the children in their care. She argues powerfully that women's lived experiences 'belong to a whole that is not of our creation' – and comments that the 'connecting fibres of this invisible institution . . . determine our relationship to our children whether we like to think so or not' (*OWB*: 277). Motherhood does not come 'naturally' to most women – no 'instinct' helps a woman face the demands placed on her by the needs of her children. In Rich's thought, the woman herself is not the problem but rather, this invisible nexus of power relations in which she – as mother – is enmeshed.

Motherhood as experience, motherhood as institution

In her analysis of motherhood, Rich identifies two strands: '*motherhood as experience*, one possible and profound experience for women, and motherhood as enforced identity and as political *institution*' in which women are seen primarily as mothers and expected to be unambivalently happy about it (*LSS*: 196–7). And to be 'different' – a non-mother, a single mother, a mother who is lesbian – is to be deviant, 'outside the law', 'abnormal'. Rich distinguishes two meanings of motherhood: 'the *potential relationship* of any woman to her powers of reproduction and to children; and the *institution*, which aims at ensuring that that potential – and all women – shall remain under male control' (*OWB*: 13). She sees the institution of mothering as systematised in political ways, as imposed on women, and as managed and organised so as to serve the interests of patriarchal social systems. As a system, it is sustained through propaganda, and maintained in and through a rigorous control of the woman's sexual and reproductive body:

> This institution – which affects each woman's personal experience – is visible in the male dispensation of birth control and abortion; the guardianship of men over children in the courts and the educational system; the subservience, through most of history, of women and children to the patriarchal father; the economic dominance of the father over the family; the usurpation of the birth process by a male medical establishment. The subjectivity of the fathers (who are also sons) has prescribed how, when, and even where women should conceive, bear, nourish, and indoctrinate their children. (*LSS*: 196)

In invoking the personal and individual experience of motherhood and setting that against motherhood as an institution, Rich identifies the maternal matrix as delineated by intractable, culturally sanctioned presumptions and coercive regulatory systems which constrain the individual mother, pressuring her to assent to specific forms of the mothering role, pre-empting her choices and limiting her potential.

The charge of biological essentialism

Rich is not suggesting that women are born to be mothers or that our biology is our destiny – far from it. Being a good mother is most emphatically not a natural, biologically determined given – rather, she argues that the imaginable domain of motherhood has been mapped and appropriated by the oppressive economies and social coercions of the patriarchal 'institution of motherhood'. Rich is at pains to stress that 'We learn, often through painful self-discipline and self-cauterization, those qualities which are supposed to be "innate" in us: patience, self-sacrifice, the willingness to repeat endlessly the small, routine chores of socializing a human being' (*OWB*: 37). In no sense is any biologically essentialist assumption made that women possess *in their natures* the qualities of nurturant caring. In Rich's thought it is a quality learned only with difficulty, often at the cost of a serious loss of self: especially the self of the writer. As she points out: 'it can be dangerously simplistic to fix upon "nurturance" as a special strength of women, which need only be released into the larger society to create a new human order' (ibid.: 283). Biology has not endowed women with an essential femininity, there is no biologically given essence that determines that the mother will be a nurturant caregiver, or be virtuous and loving towards her children. To present Rich's arguments, as Janet Sayers did in her book, *Biological Politics*, as grounded in 'the celebration of female biology and of the essential femininity to which it supposedly gives rise', is to seriously misread her work (1982: 165). Rich's arguments imply that the maternal body is lived: it is bound up in its specificity with the realms of the social and the political and is a crucial site of struggle in which psychoanalytic, sexual, technological, economic, medical, legal and other cultural institutions contest for power.

Sayers addresses her own failure to give due recognition to the importance of psychoanalytic theory in her later book *Sexual*

Contradictions (1986), yet continues to condemn Rich (as she does Irigaray) for the sin of essentialism and, in so doing, compounds the slippages of her position. Rich is again criticised for 'affirming a particular cultural representation and image of femininity . . . of woman as a plenitude of sexuality' – which seems to me to miss the point on a grand scale (1986: 47). Sayers reductively dismisses Rich's breadth, complexity and multidimensionality, in focusing on a fragment of a much larger comment when she states categorically that 'women's supposed "complicated, pain-enduring, multipleasured physicality" hardly seems a very hopeful basis on which to build resistance to their social subordination' (ibid.: 42). Well no, it wouldn't be, if that were actually what Rich was proposing.

In my reading of *Of Woman Born*, I see Rich as calling upon women to profoundly question the 'institution of motherhood', and this effort requires us to engage in a continuous, self-consciously vigilant – individual and socio-political – process of bringing to critical awareness the contradictions, ambiguities and impositions of our diverse experiences as mothers – across the globe. In individual terms, as I have suggested, it is to become open to the body's 'truth' – in order to bring to language the denials, splittings, projections, uncertainties and anguish felt – and so to work through to a realm in which such incoherences are rendered conscious and intelligible within language. In effect, the project is to find ways of encouraging incoherences into articulation *so that they may be thought*. Other, more creative potentials may then be opened up, pursued, and contested in the public realm of social, legal, economic, educational, medical and psychotherapeutic fields of expertise. This invitation to *transform thinking*, I would argue, constitutes a very different project. Rich does, most emphatically, challenge male-defined knowledges and socio-political structures in identifying the multiple ways in which they have constrained and subdued women's bodies through history and at different times, in different parts of the world.

Thinking through the body: from silence to speech

I would like to offer a fuller rendering of this idea of 'thinking through the body', as it seems to me to be of considerable importance in Rich's work. I want especially to draw attention to her questioning of patriarchal language as failing to allow 'thinking through the body', as a major theme which permeates *Of Woman Born*, and the poetry of this period. Clearly influenced by Susan Sontag, Rich offers this strong statement:

> I am convinced that 'there are ways of thinking that we don't yet know about' (Susan Sontag). I take those words to mean that many women are *even now* thinking in ways which traditional intellection denies, decries, or is unable to grasp. Thinking is an active, fluid, expanding process; intellection, 'knowing' are recapitulations of past processes. In arguing that we have by no means yet explored or understood our biological grounding, the miracle and paradox of the female body and its spiritual and political meanings, I am really asking whether women cannot begin, at last, to *think through the body*, to connect what has been so cruelly disorganised – our great mental capacities, hardly used; our highly developed tactile sense; our genius for close observation; our complicated, pain-enduring, multipleasured physicality. (*OWB*: 283–4)[3]

In Rich's thought at this time, the cognitive potentiality of our bodies has been enmeshed in systems of thought created by men whose 'fear and hatred of our bodies has often crippled our brains'. Deeply critical of male-dominated cultural forms, she sees these life-denying systems of thought as emerging from a 'death-culture of quantification, abstraction and the will to power' (*OWB*: 284). If to be male, logical and rational is to be sane, then any 'female', intuitive, poetic, sensory or 'supersensory' knowing becomes 'irrational', 'hysterical', 'madness': 'Moreover, the term "rational" relegates to its opposite term all that it refuses to deal with, and thus ends by assuming itself to be purified of the nonrational, rather than searching to identify and assimilate its own surreal or nonlinear elements' (ibid.: 62).

How to unblock the 'uncivilised', embodied word?

Influenced by Rich, and influencing Rich, Susan Griffin's thesis in *Woman and Nature* throws much light on Rich's thinking – as of lesbian-feminist thinking – in the mid-seventies. In *Woman and Nature*, Griffin set herself the task of examining patriarchal 'thought' – which she argues 'does represent itself as emotionless (objective, detached and bodiless)' and characteristically conveys the sense 'that it has found absolute truth, or at least has the authority to do so' (1984: xv–xvii). She found herself afraid of this 'paternal voice': 'It sprang out at me in the form of recognized opinion and told me that the reactions I experienced in my female body to its declarations were ridiculous (unfounded, hysterical, biased).' Only by refusing the authority and truth of the 'paternal voice' and 'going underneath logic', tuning in to 'feeling' and 'enlisting my intuition, or uncivilised self', did Susan Griffin find her way towards a mode of thinking – both 'embodied' and 'impassioned' – that is 'not so much utopian as a description of a different way of seeing'. It is precisely this impulse that informs Rich's thesis in *Of Woman Born*. The wild or 'uncivilised self' gestured towards here seems to symbolise this unspoken, excluded, otherness beyond the law – of the language of the body. It is a project that lies close to the core of Rich's thinking:

> Truly to liberate women, then, means to change thinking itself: to reintegrate what has been named the unconscious, the subjective, the emotional with the structural, the rational, the intellectual; to 'connect the prose and the passion' in E.M. Forster's phrase; and finally to annihilate those dichotomies. (*OWB*: 81)

Rich was clearly not alone in her critique of the dualisms characteristic of Western philosophic thought. Logocentrism with its dual, hierarchical oppositions organises what is thinkable within a binary system, in which the relations of authority order, categorise and guarantee meaning, and it was at the root of the problem for such diverse, spiritually aware writers as Mary Daly, Rosemary Reuther, Susan Griffin, Hélène Cixous and Luce Irigaray.

The re-visioning of mythology, spirituality and religion

In the dualistic splitting characteristic of (particularly Judao-Christian) patriarchal forms, pure woman as fertile mother is idealised; impure woman, barren woman, evil woman, is condemned. Polarising the female body into good and bad aspects has proved an intransigent defence against encountering the woman/mother in her totality:

Throughout patriarchal mythology, dream-symbolism, theology, language, two ideas flow side by side: one, that the female body is impure, corrupt, the site of discharges, bleedings, dangerous to masculinity, a source of moral and physical contamination, 'the devil's gateway'. On the other hand, as mother the woman is beneficent, sacred, pure, asexual, nourishing; and the physical potential for motherhood – that same body with its bleedings and mysteries – is her single destiny and justification in life. (*OWB*: 34)

Accepting her own anger as a mother allows for both inside and outside of her lived body to be represented in her theorising and her art. If 'Experience' can be both privately and publicly reconceptualised, anger and tenderness, despite being contradictory emotions, need not be mutually exclusive terms. This tension-filled conflict may live and breathe in her body as different aspects of her experiencing, yet both are integral to the processes and struggles of being a mother:

Anger and tenderness: my selves.
And now I can believe they breathe in me
as angels, not polarities.
Anger and tenderness: the spider's genius
to spin and weave in the same action
from her own body, anywhere –
even from a broken web. (*AWP*: 9)

The image of the spider spinning and weaving simultaneously strongly suggests the indivisibility of culture and nature, subjectivity and objectivity, social and psychological, body and mind: these are inter-implicated, in this non-dichotomous understanding of the mind/body. These few lines point to a radically subversive process. Identifying herself and other women who fall short of the nurturing ideal of conventional motherhood, Rich transgressively restores to language that which had been silenced and delegit- imised within a patriarchal culture and tradition dominated by a Christian God the Father. This culturally unacceptable anger becomes acknowledged and recognised, rather than condemned. To profoundly accept her own split 'selves' (and those of other women) is to validate and to transform each one's sensory experi- encing, her self-esteem, her sense of her own power, the meaning of her existence. From being transfixed by culturally imposed, essentialist injunctions that insist that *woman's nature is to nurture*, women may now move from a position of disempowerment and self-castigation towards a greater sense of integrity – a discursive shift has occurred that significantly permits new identifications to be made, different positions to be taken up, new inner and outer perspectives to be considered, and thus a new future may become conceivable, other potentials may become possible.

The contentious chapter in *Of Woman Born*, 'The Primacy of the Mother', was surely fuelled by the desire and the necessity 'to create ourselves anew' (*OWB*: 86). In that chapter, Rich had looked to anthropology to provide an empowering model radically other to that characteristically found within patriarchal forms. Rich was at the time profoundly influenced by Mary Daly's *Beyond God the Father* with its groundbreaking critique of patriarchal religious and cultural hierarchies. Daly had highlighted the fact that women were 'discovering more and more the androcentrism of God- language and being compelled to reject this, and beyond this, by discovering the male-centredness of the entire society which this legitimates' (1986: 38, 40). She argued further that women needed to put energy into 'the creation of new space, in which women are free to become who we are, in which there are real and significant alternatives to the prefabricated identities provided within the enclosed spaces of patriarchal institutions'. Both of these urgencies were germane to the writing of *Of Woman Born*.

In turning to anthropology, especially to the writings of Jane Harrison, Robert Briffault, Helen Diner and Elaine Morgan, the frustratingly unclear work of J.J. Bachofen, and the catalytic storytelling of Elizabeth Gould Davis, Rich had looked for a trans- formed perspective, had sought 'to imagine a wholly different way for women to exist in the world'. She was later to call for caution. Gould Davis's work she considered as 'anti-political and biological determinist' and she was to distance herself strongly from Gould's insistence that women's 'spiritual force' will lead the way: 'Since reforms are pointless, this is an invitation to drift into the future on the current of woman's presumed spiritual superiority' (*OWB*: 92).

Gould's usefulness to Rich, however, was that she affirmed women as powerful rather than negatively depicting women as victims. This was especially appealing politically as images validating female power and the female body could build confidence, could inspire and thus empower women to act in the world: 'If women were powerful once, a precedent exists; if female biology was ever once a source of power, it need not remain what it has since become: a root of powerlessness' (*OWB*: 85). Critical of Shulamith Firestone's argument in *The Dialectic of Sex*, in which she seeks through reproductive technology to free women 'from the tyranny of reproduction by every means possible', Rich finds herself focusing not so much on abandoning the biological 'givens' as on creating affirmative images to uphold a sense of the female as powerful within cultural forms (Firestone, 1979: 221). In this task she was partly inspired by images from G. Rachel Levy's *Religious Conceptions of the Stone Age* (1963), as well as from Erich Neumann's *The Great Mother* (1972), though in the chapter overall she explores and evaluates a wide range of mythological representations. She respectfully but critically assesses their different contributions and considers their value to the project of upholding a woman-centred spirituality. This effort is part of the larger political project of setting positively empowering images of women against those emanating from within God-centred and man-centred patriarchal institutions.

Matriarchy madness: reactionary utopia or sound political sense?

The complexities of thought to be found within Rich's poetry and prose were utterly overlooked in the negative critical assessments that were to follow over the next decade. Hester Eisenstein, in her book *Contemporary Feminist Thought*, suggested that following Rich, Mary Daly, Susan Griffin and others had 'brought radical feminism to a theoretical and practical impasse' (1984: xii). She worried that this line of thinking was to encourage feminism towards a matriarchal utopianism having at its heart a reactionary concept, that of

> the intrinsic moral superiority of women. As advanced by these writers, the concept is triply problematic: in its implicit attribution of female superiority to physiological causes; in its renunciation of rationality and clarity as fundamentally male and therefore flawed; and in its pessimistic depiction of women as the innocent, passive, and powerless victims of male violence.

This 'weakness' within radical feminism Eisenstein attributed to the 'divorce from Marxism and the political Left, a consistent emphasis on psychology at the expense of economic factors; and a false universalism that addresses itself to all women, with insufficient regard for differences of race, class and culture'. Rich was clearly 'not guilty' of these charges, though many have argued that in her emphasis on the body of woman, she comes close to committing biological essentialism. She has never renounced rationality as male. Rather, she has claimed the intellect as also female. And her excursion into anthropology was undoubtedly undertaken in order to uphold a sense of women as powerful – as anything but passive – so that women could lift themselves out of feeling victimised. Certainly the great value to women of this spiritual trajectory within feminism lies precisely in its power to inspire, to lift self-esteem, to empower from within, but I do not see Rich as in any sense upholding 'the intrinsic moral superiority of women'.

Sally R. Binford in her article 'Myths and Matriarchies' (1979), strongly resisted the 'Mother Goddess/Matriarchy Madness' which she saw as sweeping academia, in which 'the faith of the New Feminist Fundamentalism' carries a certainty that is 'stronger than reason' (1979: 146–7). By this time, Rich herself was beginning to take 'a good hard look' at women's spirituality, noting how much of it is just 'a fad', 'the same old stuff that is being sold and bought all over the country, by all kinds of people.

They are apolitical people, antifeminist, and certainly counter-revolutionary' (Packwood, 1981: 14). This materialist mode of criticism was ultimately to challenge Rich to rethink her position in relation to Marxist feminist analysis, and she leaves behind this fascinating but, in terms of Rich's later thinking, problematic area of concern.

Though she was ambivalently drawn to the idea of a prehistoric matriarchal period, when 'not a handful, but most women were using their capacities to the utmost', Rich was, from the first, highly suspicious of the 'seductive' lure of ideas of a lost golden age, and voiced her unease about 'the limitations of our sources' very strongly (*OWB*: 85–6). Her search, rather, is marked by the desire to 'call up before women a different condition than the one we have known, to prime the imagination of women living today to conceive of other modes of existence' (*OWB*: 91).[4] She sought to fire women's desires, to imagine other possibilities than those offered within patriarchal cultures, and to focus women's energies to work towards a transformed future. For Rich it was a political rather than a religiously motivated project, and it was thus easier for her than for others more spiritually committed to pull back from this particular trajectory of her thought. However, her aims then were valid, and still have validity, especially in the field of theology, as in women's therapy and spirituality generally. She had wanted to identify a potential horizon towards which women could aspire, without defining or delimiting that future. Desire, need, longing, after all, is always future oriented. And yet the project of spirituality can also be motivated by the desire *not* to be constrained within patriarchal thought forms, not to be bound up within male-centred economies of desire. Ten years on, and having become highly suspicious of a radical feminist spirituality which is sometimes indistinguishable from 'a New Age blur of the-personal-for-its-own-sake', Rich was to veer away from what she saw as the individualism, the psychologising, and the apolitical idealisation of the nurturant feminine within feminist spirituality: 'I never wished this book to lend itself to the sentimentalization of women or of women's nurturant or spiritual capacity' (*OWB*: x, xxxiv). Her definition of patriarchy had by this time undergone re-vision, nonetheless it is still a valuable concept and ought not to be used as a 'catchall' (ibid.: xxiii). And so, in the 1986 Introduction, we find Rich's new formulation of her political critique levels itself at 'old idea systems' rather than 'men', it becomes specific to time and place, and shows sensitivity to economic and racial dimensions:

> Patriarchy is a concrete and useful concept. Whether it is considered as a phenomenon dating from capitalism or as part of the precapitalist history of many peoples, which must also be confronted under existing socialisms, it is now widely recognised as a name for an identifiable sexual hierarchy. We are not in danger of losing our grasp on patriarchy as a major form of domination parallel and interconnected to race and class. (*OWB*: xxiii–xxiv)

Thus, in the intervening ten years, Rich was able to stand back from herself and be critical of the omissions of (her own?) white middle-class feminist thought, was ready herself to identify the gaps over which an earlier Rich – and an earlier theory – had glossed. She notes particularly that 'the mystique of woman's moral superiority (deriving from nineteenth-century ideals of middle-class female chastity and of the maternal) can lurk even where the pedestal has been kicked down' (*OWB*: xxiv).

Developing a politics of diversity

Not just sexual difference but differences of all kinds begin to be addressed – for Rich's self-searching, holistic critical method does not fail to consider the other/Other in all dimensions. As we have seen, the refusal of dualistic thinking is fundamental. Rich seeks to permit different thinking in the larger global sense, in affirming the existence not only of women, but also all subordinated humanity:

> The rejection of the dualism, of the positive–negative polarities between which most of our intellectual training has taken place, has been an undercurrent of feminist thought. And, rejecting them, we affirm the existence of all those who have through the centuries been negatively defined: not only women, but the 'untouchable', the 'unmanly', the 'nonwhite', the 'illiterate': the 'invisible'. (*OWB*: 64)

This passage is rooted in a concept of difference that points towards a globally relevant formulation, one that may have veered away from a formulaic economic and class-based analysis of Marxist thought but which is no less concerned with those made 'other' to the affluent, educated, able, white or culturally dominant heterosexual male.

But is it enough? Quoting from Rich's grand positional statement 'The repossession by women of our bodies will bring far more essential change to human society than the seizing of the means of production by workers' (*OWB*: 285), Rachel Blau DuPlessis had asked, in 1978,

> Is body organisation more potent, more potentially revolutionary, more 'essential' than economic organisation? Vases, faces: I say yes, I say no. Is body organisation as others appropriate it the material basis for the oppression of women? Does repossession of our bodies occur as an act of will and mind, or as an act of social transformation? If this repossession is a spiritual act of definition alone, I feel it will not have sufficient momentum: for as patriarchy is affirmed economically, politically, culturally, the overthrow of a patriarchal system must be affirmed in legal, political, economic spheres. (Blau DuPlessis, 1978: 400)

In the 1986 introduction to *Of Woman Born*, Rich does profoundly reconsider her earlier radical feminist position. She is still deeply committed to the belief that 'the free exercise by all women of sexual and procreative choice will catalyze enormous social transformations', but now she will add that, for women as for certain men, 'the claim to personhood; the claim to share justly in the products of our labor, not to be used merely as an instrument, a role, a womb, a pair of hands or a back, or a set of fingers; to participate fully in the decisions of our workplace, our community; to speak for ourselves in our own right' are just as important (*OWB*: xvii–xviii). Her rereading of 'the revolutionary thinkers of the nineteenth and early twentieth centuries' – she mentions Trotsky and Marx – has by the mid-eighties led to this crucial re-vision of her position (*WIFT*: 45). Likening women's 'right to choose' to the nineteenth-century reforms of the Factory Acts, she argues that 'procreative choice is for women an equivalent of the demand for the legally limited working day' (*OWB*: xviii).

The Rise of the Christian Right

The intervening ten years saw the rise of the Christian Right and the 'Declaration of National Moral Emergency' by fundamentalist ministers and others on the Right, as a reaction to feminist activism around the ERA (Equal Rights Amendment), abortion rights and gay rights. Charlene Spretnak had noted in 1982 the kind of language used in these ultra-conservative declarations: 'feminists are "moral perverts", "godless humanists" and "enemies of every decent society"'.[5] At the time, aligning itself alongside the fundamentalist Christian Right, the Republican Party's political programme aimed to take 'nearly all the public funding out of social services [which are supported by 'socialistic Christian liberals' and 'demonic secular humanists'] and put this money into a greatly increased defence budget, plus large tax cuts'.[6]

By 1984, the 'Moral Majority' leader Jerry Falwell had condemned the 'decadence' of abortion and gay rights, and President Reagan, in his State of the Union address, had linked his election to 'a crusade for "renewal," "a spiritual revival" in America, denounced the "tragedy of abortion", and was to state that "families stand at the center of our society"' (Pratt, 1984: 38). The year 1984 saw abortion clinics being bombed by the Army of God, and the Reagan budget paid '$555 more to the military and $88 less to poor children and their mothers'. What Rich was to term in 1986 'the war against the poor', had begun (*OWB*: xiv). So too had the 'assault on women's right to safe, affordable abortion' (ibid.: xv).

These arguments are still in full spate, and though Rich could not have foretold these developments, it is plain that the work of women striving for social change, whether in secular life or within the more radical churches and synagogues, is crucially important if women in the US are not to lose much of the ground they have gained through the last two decades.

I have not exhausted the complexity of *Of Woman Born*. Limitations of space prevent me from entering into arguments around abortion, reproductive technology, midwifery and childbirth.[7] In the next chapter, I will be considering the question of difference, specifically the difference of being lesbian, as a principle for organising politically. Rich's critique of 'Compulsory

Heterosexuality' and her notion of the 'Lesbian Continuum' come under fire from critics. Theory leaves identity politics behind. It becomes increasingly difficult to develop an integrated political practice. Rich's commitment to radical complexity urges her towards a politics capable of addressing far wider issues, just as accepting diversity and difference more fully demands a new, global politics.

Notes

1 The years 1974–76 when *Of Woman Born* was being written, saw the publication of Juliet Mitchell's *Psychoanalysis and Feminism* (1974), Jean Baker Miller's *Psychoanalysis and Women* (1974) and Linda Gordon's major treatise: *Woman's Body, Woman's Right: A Social History of Birth Control in America* (1976).

2 Feminists in France (and bilingual Americans) welcomed the publication of radical psychoanalyst and philosopher Luce Irigaray's vast and important doctoral thesis, *Speculum de l'autre femme* in 1974. In this now classic book, Irigaray offers a major rereading of Freud's essay 'Femininity' and his other writings on women, a devastating critique of Plato and therefore of Western philosophy and she also, as did Mary Daly before her, raised the question of woman's relation to a male God. This book was followed shortly after by Hélène Cixous and Catherine Clement's *La Jeune Neé (The Newly Born Woman)* in 1975. Though Rich did not read these French writers, they were published around the same time as *Of Woman Born*. She did, however, read Wittig's *Les Guérillères* and *The Lesbian Body*, and in 1976 met and became friends with Christine Delphy, and read some of her work.

3 Rich quotes from Susan Sontag, *Styles of Radical Will*: see *OWB*: 281.

4 This comment was actually made by Rich about the work of Elizabeth Gould Davis. I think it is true of her own work also, which is why I suggest that her work is 'marked' by this desire.

5 'The Christian Right's "Holy War" against Feminism', in Spretnak (1994: 470–1). Spretnak quotes from George Romney, speaking of ERA supporters during an interview with Harry Cook (Knight-Ridder Wire Release, 19 December 1979); Tim LaHaye's pamphlet and book *The Battle for the Minds*, and Meldrim Thompson, Jr., national chairman of the Conservative Caucus, quoted by M. Eileen McEachern, 'Don't Call Me Ms.', *Boston Globe Sunday Magazine*, 12 March 1978.

6 Spretnak quotes Howard Phillips, from an article by Alan L. Otten in the *Wall Street Journal*, 29 May 1975; and John T. Dolan, quoted in Myra MacPherson, 'The New Right Brigade', *Washington Post*, 10 August 1980. Spretnak, p. 471.

7 Readers interested in Rich's consideration of the relation between mother and daughter, and the arguments around essentialism, may wish to refer to my earlier book, *Impertinent Voices* (Yorke, 1991) where I explore these aspects more fully.

4 Lesbian Identity, Compulsory Heterosexuality and 'The Common Woman'

'We came together in a common
fury of direction
barely mentioning difference
(what drew our finest hairs
to fire
the deep, difficult troughs
unvoiced) . . .

Adrienne Rich, 'For Memory' (*AWP*: 21)

This chapter focuses on questions of political identity, specifically lesbian identity, during the late seventies and early eighties. Through her notion of a 'lesbian continuum', Rich attempts to collapse the difference – that is, the dualistic dichotomy – between heterosexual and lesbian women. She invites women to unite in the interests of all women through forging a political 'identity' that could encompass all shades of difference between the poles of the duality. This attempt flounders in controversy and theory moves on to leave this apparently outmoded identity politics stranded. Even as identity politics is dying, a new politics of diversity is being created from the productive tensions between lesbian and heterosexual, as well as between Black and white, feminisms. Nonetheless, debate still centres around questions of identity. Which version of 'woman' should inform political strategy? Indeed, should lesbians call themselves 'women' at all?

The 1976 prose essay, 'It Is the Lesbian in Us . . .', celebrates the word 'lesbian', and identifies the '"primary intensity" between women' that for Rich marked the identity 'lesbian' (*LSS*: 202). To be lesbian is to be a 'self-chosen woman', to be a 'woman who has said "no" to the fathers'. It is to be a woman 'who gravitates towards strong women', who refuses to obey, and who is driven to 'feel imaginatively, render in language, grasp, the full connection between woman and woman' (ibid.: 201). In this essay, Rich speaks of a 'complex, demanding realm of linguistic and relational distinctions' which must be explored in order to grasp our experience as lesbians'(ibid.: 202). This combative political aim gives impetus to the courageous acts of naming and defining of the coming-out poems collected in *The Dream of a Common Language*. This collection was written contemporaneously to *Of Woman Born* and the themes of the poems and the book resonate powerfully each with the other.

The 'concept' of the 'Lesbian in Us' is further developed in the controversial essay: 'Compulsory Heterosexuality and Lesbian Existence' which was written in part 'to encourage heterosexual feminists to examine heterosexuality as a political institution which disempowers women' (*BBP*: 23). This essay, with its emphasis on 'the depth and breadth of woman identification and woman bonding' as a 'politically activating impulse, not simply a validation of personal lives', also provides an intellectual grounding for many of the poems of this period. As Rich put it, she wanted 'some bridge over the gap between *lesbian* and *feminist*. I wanted, at the very least, for feminists to find it less possible to read, write, or teach from a perspective of unexamined heterocentricity' (ibid.: 23–4).

Lesbian existence and the lesbian continuum

Bridging the gap for Rich involved inventing the new terms *lesbian existence* and *lesbian continuum*. *Lesbian existence* was to suggest

'both the fact of the historical presence of lesbians and our continuing creation of the meaning of that existence'; and the *lesbian
continuum* was to include

> a range – through each woman's life and throughout history – of
> woman-identified experience, not simply the fact that a woman has had
> or consciously desired genital sexual experience with another woman.
> If we expand it to embrace many more forms of primary intensity
> between and among women, including the sharing of a rich inner life,
> the bonding against male tyranny, the giving and receiving of practical
> and political support . . . we begin to grasp breadths of female history
> and psychology which have lain out of reach as a consequence of lim-
> ited, mostly clinical, definitions of *lesbianism*. (*BBP*: 51–2)

But these distinctions have proved problematic. Rich's lesbo-
centric attempt to rethink the heterosexual–lesbian dichotomy into
a continuum risked being viewed as a kind of co-optation which
could fail to fully respect the differences between those who do
take the risks of lesbian commitment to sexualised attachment
between women, and those who don't. Lesbians who make the
'deliberate choice, the exercising of a particular kind of courage
and the taking of certain risks' in their erotic lives need to be distinguished from women whose affectional bonds with their female
friends do not include that commitment (Raymond, 1986: 17). In
considering Rich's position, Janice Raymond was uneasy, and drew
attention to her 'gnawing intuition that this affirmation is logically
incorrect, morally short-changing to women who are Lesbians and
patronising to women who are not Lesbians' (ibid.: 16). She saw
Rich's attempt to view heterosexual women's attachment to other
women in the bonds of friendship as part of the lesbian continuum
as 'false inclusion' (ibid.: 18). Janice Raymond's word gyn/affec-
tion, is perhaps a more appropriate term, in that it can include
lesbians as well as those who would not define themselves as such,
but is rarely used in practice.[1] Martha E. Thompson's suggestion,
in her elaboration of Rich's paper, that 'important relationships
with women are transformed into reciprocal and primary ones
when women come together to change their collective conditions,
not just to share their personal experiences', seems romantic, even
utopian (Thompson, 1981: 793). Underlying all of these attempts to
formulate a 'common language' within feminism is a passionate

desire, grounded in the primary intensity of attachment, to create a political sense of mutuality, commonality, community and resistance which ignores the vast range of differences between women.

The critique of heterosexuality

Rich did not invent the concept of 'heterocentricity': in 1971, a 12-woman collective defining themselves as lesbian-feminist separatists, founded the paper *The Furies*. In that paper, reprinted in Charlotte Bunch's 'Not For Lesbians Only', they set out their political concerns: not simply fighting for civil rights for lesbians, nor the promotion of lesbian culture, but the recognition that 'Lesbian feminist politics is a political critique of the institution and ideology of heterosexuality as a cornerstone of male supremacy. It is an extension of the analysis of sexual politics to an analysis of sexuality itself as an institution. It is a commitment to women as a political group which is the basis of a political/economic strategy leading to power for women, not just an alternative community' (Bunch, 1981: 68). Like Bunch, Rich argues that 'compulsory heterosexuality' is another political institution to be set alongside the other institutions 'by which women have traditionally been controlled – patriarchal motherhood, economic exploitation, the nuclear family' (*BBP*: 24). Identifying the methods by which male power is maintained, Rich puts together an overwhelmingly convincing list, ranging from physical brutality to the withholding of 'large areas of the society's knowledge and cultural attainments': including the physical and/or emotional brutality of clitoridectomy, rape, battery, sexual abuse, pornography, harassment: she scans across a range of social, legal and economic abuses of various kinds, and summons a vast array of well-respected feminist critiques to support her case (*BBP*: 38). Working daily with women who are fighting back from such abuses, I can say that the distress of women injured by such multiform abuses is incalculable and should not be underestimated by those unfamiliar with the scene of therapy. Cora Kaplan's dismissive critique of Rich's theoretical stance is one I find unhelpful and inaccurate, particularly her suggestion that in Rich's thought

> heterosexuality is a part of a chain of gender-specific tortures, both medical and conjugal: hysterectomy, clitoridectomy, battering, rape and imprisonment are all elaborations of the sadistic act of penetration itself, penetration the socially valorised symbol of violence against women. Men use these torments to shore up their own subjectivity. Their pleasure in them is a confirmation of male power. Pornography, in this analysis is emblematic of all male sexuality, the violent fantasy behind the tenderest act of intercourse. (Kaplan, 1986: 52)

This to me constitutes a wilful and in itself reductionist misreading of Rich's thesis in 'Compulsory Heterosexuality', and it misses the point on a grand scale. The ramifications of cultural power are not to be equated to an act of penetration, however sadistic. Nor is pornography, whatever relevance it has to male sexuality, 'the violent fantasy behind the tenderest acts of intercourse' in Rich's thought – not here, nor elsewhere in her work. Men, as is very apparent in therapeutic work, actually do use their power against others – weaker or more feminine, male or female – who are socially less powerful than themselves, to keep them in their place, to shore up a fragile identity, and to confirm to themselves that they do have the right, within patriarchal cultures, to exercise that power. Just as, of course, women can also misuse their power to the (vastly lesser) extent that they have power within patriarchal cultures.

A more supportive Sheila Jeffreys argues that 'Heterosexuality is not indicted, only the force necessary to get women to participate' (Jeffreys, 1990: 297). As I have suggested, Rich has not indicated any problem with what Kaplan calls 'the tenderest acts'. Rather, she denounces the violent fantasies and brutal acts which are perpetrated by men wielding their power, and which function forcefully to organise male supremacy. As Sheila Jeffreys has also pointed out, 'heterosexuality is constructed by various means, including force, and relies upon the prevention of the bonding of women' (ibid.: 299). Rich's analysis, in fact, addresses itself to the crucial task of creating a community of resistance, inviting both lesbians and heterosexual feminists to bond together in recognising manifest prescription, coercion, compulsion, colonisation and other serious misuses of power within the institutions of heterosexuality. She strongly urges heterosexual women to take 'a critical stance toward the ideology which *demands* heterosexuality' (*BBP*: 25).

> there is a real, identifiable system of heterosexual propaganda, of defining women as existing for the sexual use of men, which goes beyond 'sex role' or 'gender' stereotyping or 'sexist imagery' to include a vast number of verbal and non-verbal messages. And this I call 'control of consciousness.' The possibility of a woman who does not exist sexually for men – the lesbian possibility – is buried, erased, occluded, distorted, misnamed, and driven underground. (*BBP*: 71–2).

The notion of 'control of consciousness' now has a curiously sixties ring, but signals Rich's concern to counter those discourses which set out to objectify women, to intimidate us, to program our thinking, and place women as existing for the use of men.

The challenge of Black feminist thought

Being 'mothered' by a Black nurse as a child, working in the SEEK program during the sixties, and being in long-term partnership with Afro-Caribbean Michelle Cliff (from 1976), particularly influenced Rich's political choices during the seventies. At the same time, Rich continually developed her reading of Black writers. She read Toni Cade Bambara's *The Black Woman* (1970), and Michele Russell's 'An Open Letter to the Academy' (1981) – one aimed at a Black audience, the other towards white women in the universities – and both of these had a considerable impact on her thinking. Barbara Smith's essay 'Toward a Black Feminist Criticism', with its powerful critique of Black male critics, and of white feminists Elaine Showalter, Ellen Moers and Patricia Meyer Spacks among others, identifies the many omissions and distortions that can ensue from racism, ignorance and insensitivity. In calling for 'a developed body of Black feminist political theory' to inform literary critical analysis, Smith comments: 'I would at least like to see in print white women's acknowledgement of the contradictions of who and what are being left out of their research and writing'.[2] These influences were formative in Rich's decision to align her position with newly emergent Black feminist groups which had as their aim the formation of a broader-based political movement. The publication of 'A Black Feminist Statement' by the Combahee River Collective (date of writing, 1977) marks a moment when Black feminists saw as their particular task 'the development of integrated analysis and practice based upon the fact that the major systems of oppression are interlocking' (Moraga and Andalzúa, 1981: 210). They committed themselves to organising around an identity politics: 'We believe that the most profound and potentially the most radical politics come directly out of our own identity, as opposed to working to end somebody else's oppression' (ibid.: 212). This group were also to address further difficult questions relating to feminism in the Black movement as well as racism in the white feminist movement.

Radical lesbian-feminist philosopher Mary Daly had drawn attention to many important issues around language and difference in her Gyn/Ecology (1978). She also highlighted the crucial political importance of acknowledging difference: 'Recognizing the chasms of differences among sister Voyagers is coming to understand the terrifying terrain through which we must travel together and apart' (Daly, 1979: 382). Her work, however, emerging as it did from within white feminist theorising, evidences many of the blanks of that positioning: the unawareness, the speaking for others, the unconscious racism that overlooks the non-participation of non-Western women in feminist theorising and debate. Rich was to take Daly to task, in 'Notes for a Magazine: What Does Separatism Mean?' (1981), for her inward focus and for her emphasis on the 'terrifying' nature of difference, in commenting 'surely not all differences are terrifying'. Daly was also publicly challenged in 'An Open Letter to Mary Daly' (1979), by Black lesbian-feminist Audre Lorde, for her 'assumption that the herstory and myth of white women is the legitimate and sole herstory and myth of all women' (Lorde, 1984: 69). Like many other white feminists at the time, Daly was, as Lorde comments, 'unable to hear Black women's words, or to maintain dialogue with us' and did not respond to Lorde's letter (ibid.: 66). How could the movement establish commonality when confronting racial and other differences was apparently so difficult?

In the interests of developing a stronger sense of women-identified connection, the issues of racial difference, class difference, religious difference – awareness of othernesses of all kinds – needed to be addressed, as a political imperative. If attempting to forge a sense of the mutual (non-dominant) interdependency of women meant raw and powerful – and not always successful – contact across differences, then finding new ways of being meant finding real courage to traverse 'the terrain of the Otherworld Journey' (Daly, 1979: 411). Yet, despite her criticisms, Lorde acknowledges her debt to Daly in the 'Open Letter. . . .' Articulating her own, strongly worded version of the women-identified, aware politics of difference, in these words of Lorde's we can hear echoes of Daly's rhetorical flourishes:

> Advocating the mere tolerance of difference between women is the grossest reformism. It is a total denial of the creative function of difference in our lives. Difference must be not merely tolerated, but seen as a fund of necessary polarities between which our creativity can spark like a dialectic. Only then does the necessity for interdependency become unthreatening. (Lorde, 1984: 111)

The 'interdependency' of (and the difference between) these three lesbian feminists, Daly, Lorde and Rich – 'who choose to be present to each other' at this time – is striking (Daly, 1979: xii). And while there is no doubt that Rich deeply respected Audre Lorde's strong, political voice, she also struggled with her forceful pronouncements. In 'An Interview: Audre Lorde and Adrienne Rich', she was to comment:

> I take seriously the spaces between us that difference has created, that racism has created . . .
> I've had great resistance to some of your perceptions. They can be very painful to me. Perceptions about what goes on between us, what goes on between Black and white people, what goes on between Black and white women. So it's not that I can just accept your perceptions unblinkingly. Some of them are very hard for me. But I don't want to deny them. I know I can't afford to. (Lorde, 1984: 104–5)

And so, publicly and privately, lesbians are by the late seventies finding themselves both coming together and falling apart in trying to construct a diverse woman-centred identity as a presence within language so as to create a rallying point for challenging multiform oppressions.

The radical complexity of a global feminist movement

Rich strives to provide that rallying point, in attempting to create a fusion of lesbianism and feminism, and she commits herself to the belief that 'a militant and pluralistic lesbian/feminist movement is potentially the greatest force in the world today for a complete transformation of society and of our relation to all life' (*LSS*: 226). Condemning 'a simplistic dyke separatism', Rich refuses the lesbian-separatist position that would withdraw 'from the immense, burgeoning diversity of the global women's movement' (ibid.: 227). She also condemns the disturbing tendency to police other women as a defensive strategy which, in insisting on consensus, denies diversity and difference: 'I believe it is a temptation into sterile "correctness", into powerlessness, an escape from radical complexity'. And that radical complexity recognises that 'we come from many pasts: out of the Left, out of the ghetto, out of the holocaust, out of the churches, out of marriage, out of the "gay" movement, out of the closet, out of the darker closet of long-term suffocation of our love of women' (ibid.: 229).

The heroic and ordinary 'common woman'

In *A Wild Patience Has Taken Me this Far*, Rich curves into a further elaboration of her urgent political concern to consolidate woman-identification: that of identifying 'the resourceful, heroic coping of ordinary women everywhere' (*AWP, FDF*; *LSS*: 263). In her poetry, as in her politics, she embarks on a process of retrieval 'which looks with fresh eyes on all that has been trivialised, devalued, forbidden or silenced in female history', and which seeks to counter '*gynephobia*' – the 'male contempt and loathing for women and for women's bodies' – by an appeal to the concept, derived from Judy Grahn, of the 'Common Woman':

> The 'Common Woman' is far more than a class description. What is 'common' in and to women is the intersection of oppression and strength, damage and beauty. It is, quite simply, the *ordinary* in women which will 'rise' in every sense of the word – spiritually and in activism.

For us, to be 'extraordinary' or 'uncommon' is to fail. History has been embellished with 'extraordinary', 'exemplary', 'uncommon', and of course 'token' women whose lives have left the rest unchanged. The 'common woman' is in fact the embodiment of the extraordinary will-to-survival in millions of obscure women. (*LSS*: 255)

Not wishing to idealise or romanticise, Rich, in this gesture towards materialist feminism, celebrates the 'common woman', and eschews the temptation to valorise extraordinary or uncommon women. Defining 'common' in constructivist terms as an *intersection* of 'oppression and strength, damage and beauty', Rich constructs a contradictory 'identity' for 'common' women, and so her 'ordinary' women occupy a temporal and spatial *position* within language. Nowhere does she argue in essentialist terms, as does Judith Clavir, that 'one woman's experience is all women's experience, because all women have a bond which is eternal, biological and historical' (Clavir, 1979: 404–5). Rather, as her defining focus, she invents this conglomerate, future-oriented figuration which celebrates the 'embodiment of the extraordinary *will to survival* in millions of obscure women' (my emphasis) – survival is the goal, and the process of working towards 'survival' profoundly informs the ground of her philosophy.

But can this abstract *'will to survival'* be 'embodied'? Is the 'common woman' also a universalising metaphor – albeit an expedient, future-oriented metaphor providing a locational point of affinity as a unifying political principle? And does her call to repossess the body not lock her into a biologistic essentialism? Well, yes and no.

The charge of essentialism

Rich's characteristic strategy of confounding dualistic thinking has also confused her critics into denouncing the essentialism of her thinking. In fact, a both/and, body/mind holism confounds any either/or categorisation of her work. As in Irigaray's work, we can identify a double gesture: 'on one side, a "global" politics that seeks to address the problem of women's universal oppression, and on the other side', in Diana Fuss's words, 'a "local" politics that will address the specificity and complexity of each woman's particular situation' (Fuss, 1989: 68–9). Thus a multiform trajectory informs this politics: women are not a definable group with a common essence and identity, and yet there are 'millions of obscure women' whose 'ordinary' subjection *as women*, will inform their activism, and spiritually, their 'will-to-survive'. It is essential to note the predictive mode in Rich's phrase 'the ordinary in women which will "rise"', for this is not a definition of 'woman', but an anticipation of an as yet unrealised potentiality to be developed. Developing the potential of 'ordinary' women is a horizon or goal with which many could identify, an inspirational political focus to gather women's desires and energy towards working for specific local change on a global scale.

Perhaps to find some clarity, we need to ask of Rich's work – does it slide into an essentialist belief in 'the real, true essence of things, the invariable and fixed properties which define the "whatness" of a given entity'? – in other words, does this category the 'common woman' identify the original, the true, the authentic 'woman', leaving out all who would fall outside of that category (Fuss, 1989: xi)? Diana Fuss has argued that

> essentialism is typically defined in opposition to difference; the doctrine of essence is viewed as precisely that which seeks to deny or annul the very radicality of difference. The opposition is a helpful one in that it reminds us that a complex system of cultural, social, psychical and historical differences, and not a set of pre-existent human essences, position and constitute the subject. (ibid.: xii)

Given Rich's very strong focus on the global differences between women, on heterogeneity, on cultural and racial diversity, it would be hard to see her as an 'essentialist' writer. Rich does not assume that there is a true, transhistorical essence of being a woman, or of being a lesbian. Politically, a hope that runs through *A Wild Patience Has Taken Me This Far* is that a necessarily materialist focus on specific, historical contexts will create a feminism 'which looks with fresh eyes on all that has been trivialised, devalued, forbidden, or silenced in female history' (*LSS*: 263).

The retrieval of women's history

This retrieval does not mean being uncritical of women of the past. Asking Gerda Lerner's question: 'what would history be like if it were seen through the eyes of women and ordered by values they define?' involves making an attempt to become aware of the distortions and misrepresentations of different positions, recognising 'the manifold and varied experiences of millions of women' and making a critical reassessment of the significance of their contributions (Lerner, 1977: xxi–xxii).

We can identify a local, historically specific, nuanced awareness informing the politics and the poetry that explores complex variations of experience among women of different classes and races. And, far from claiming a necessary, transhistorical bond between women, the poetry attests to very shocking and unfathomable differences. In 'For Ethel Rosenberg', 'killed in the electric chair June 19, 1953', Rich brings before us the betrayal and abandonment of Ethel by her mother and her sister:

> . . . if I imagine her at all
> I have to imagine first
> the pain inflicted on her   by women
>
> *her mother testifies against her*
> *her sister-in-law testifies against her*
> and how she sees it . . . (*FDF*: 289)

Rich's radical complexity is no less than this level of empathic understanding: the recognition of another's being as separate, and another's experience as not like our own, yet still being receptive and respecting of their position, even when their position would disallow ours:

> if I dare imagine her surviving
> I must be fair to what she must have lived through
> I must allow her to be at last
>
> political in her ways   not in mine
> her urgencies perhaps   impervious to mine
> defining revolution as she defines it . . . (*FDF*: 290)

This impetus to explore radical complexity, so as to connect emotionally and politically with other women, becomes an essential part of negotiating difference.

Are lesbians 'women' anyway

'Compulsory Heterosexuality' had been written on request from the journal *Signs*, in 1978, as a response to the erasure of lesbian existence in articles published there. The same year saw Monique Wittig give her presentation 'The Straight Mind' at the MLA Conference in New York (Wittig, 1992). Monique Wittig's work was to cut right across the trajectory of Rich's work and her arguments were, ultimately, to transform the shape of feminist politics. As concerned to make visible and to examine lesbian existence as Rich, Wittig's critique grounded itself in a recognition of the power of heterosexual thinking to constitute a notion of difference and otherness as a prerequisite to domination:

> straight society is based on the necessity of the different/other at every level. . . . But what is the different/other if not the dominated? For heterosexual society is the society which not only oppresses lesbians and gay men, it oppresses many different/others, it oppresses all women and many categories of men, all those who are in the position of the dominated. To constitute a difference and to control it is an 'act of power, since it is essentially a normative act . . . One has to be socially dominant to succeed in it' [quoting from Faugeron and Robert (1978)] (ibid.: 28–9)

Wittig goes on to argue: 'If we, as lesbians and gay men, continue to speak of ourselves and to conceive of ourselves as women and as men, we are instrumental in maintaining heterosexuality' (ibid.: 30). Logically, if lesbians are truly outside the heterosexual contract, it becomes 'incorrect to say that lesbians associate, make love, live with women, for "woman" has meaning only in heterosexual systems of thought and heterosexual economic systems. Lesbians are not women' (ibid.: 32). In her 'materialist feminist' approach to women's oppression, Wittig pushed her argument even further in stating in 'One Is Not Born a Woman' (1981) that 'not only is there no natural group "women" (we lesbians are living proof of it), but as individuals as well we question "woman", which for us, as for Simone de Beauvoir, is only a myth'.

Wittig was to abandon the term 'woman' and would look towards 'a political transformation of key concepts, that is, of the concepts which are strategic for us'. She brings to the forefront of political analysis contradictions with which Rich had clearly grappled in 'Twenty-One Love Poems', and her other poetry and theory of this period. Wittig's provocative arguments stunned and disrupted the entire movement and her premises ultimately challenged the very ground of radical feminist thinking. Rich did not read *The Straight Mind* until after she had written 'Compulsory Heterosexuality', and so I write with a sense of Wittig's arguments as poised to transform radical feminist theory, when she made her shocking assertion that 'Lesbians are not women . . .' (ibid.: 9–10).

As Sue Wilkinson and Celia Kitzinger argue in their recent book *Representing the Other*, 'the notion of who and what Others are (what they are like, the attributes assigned them, the sorts of lives they are supposed to lead) is intimately related to "our" notion of who and what "we" are. That is, "we" use the Other to define ourselves: "we" understand ourselves in relation to what "we" are *not*' (1996: 8). The voices of white feminists in the late seventies were dominant within feminism: they sought to establish a sense of commonality between women, to create the 'we' of feminism, but in their unawareness of this dynamic they were also complicit in silencing and delegitimising other voices not the same as 'ours'. I want to consider now how Rich negotiates this difficult territory.

Forging a politics which can respect diversity and difference

In 'Disloyal to Civilization: Feminism, Racism, Gynephobia' (1978), Rich examines what 'black and white feminists have in common', in her effort to 'carry my thoughts on feminism and racism beyond the confines of my own mind' (*LSS*: 279). Urging caution in making attempts to 'grasp' racism 'as an intellectual or theoretical concept', she warns us not to 'move too fast', for then 'we lose touch with the feelings black women are trying to describe to us, their lived experience *as women*' (ibid.: 281). The (feeling-body) contact and connection is crucial. 'Emotional apprehension', which springs from a 'synthesis of reflection and feeling, personal struggle and critical thinking', is 'at the core of feminist process' (ibid.: 304). The concept of the 'common woman' demands that white feminists lose their solipsism:

> As women we need to develop a language in which to describe the forms that directly affect our relations with each other. I believe that white feminists today, raised white in a racist society, are often ridden with *white solipsism* – not the consciously held *belief* that one race is inherently superior to all others, but a tunnel-vision which simply does not see nonwhite experience or existence as precious or significant, unless in spasmodic, impotent guilt-reflexes, which have little or no long-term, continuing momentum or political usefulness. I believe also that we have been ridden with *mythic misperceptions* of black women and other women of color, and that these misperceptions have flourished in the combined soil of racism and gynephobia, the subjectivity of patriarchy. (ibid.: 306)

Indeed, a new language is needed to describe the necessary inner and outer processes of re-visioning history from a feminist point of view. 'Experience' as such is always interpreted in and through language, and 'radical complexity' demands that we approach the ground of knowledge production with an awareness of the blinkers, the tunnel vision, the solipsisms and the 'mythic misperceptions' of our position.

'Experience' in a constructivist era

Rich does not presume that to write of 'experience' from a female point of view allows us to privilege as 'authentic' or 'real' or non-oppressive our perceptions of women of history, yet, at the same time, she is reluctant to foreclose the questions posed by real, material existence, and the body. I find Theresa De Lauretis's post-post-structuralist formulation helpful here, in seeing 'experience' as 'an ongoing process by which subjectivity is constructed semiotically and historically' (De Lauretis, 1984: 182). This holistic formulation comes close to describing Rich's multidirectional strategy in that it does not leave historical experience out of the picture, but neither does it privilege 'experience' as either shared, authoritative, or necessarily in possession of the Truth. In no sense is a common experience being proposed that could provide a common ground through which to politicise the notion of the identity 'woman'. As Judith Butler suggests in *Gender Trouble*, decentring the defining institutions of phallogocentrism and compulsory heterosexuality requires us to ask: 'What new shape of politics emerges when identity as a common ground no longer constrains the discourse on feminist politics? And to what extent does the effort to locate a common identity as the foundation for a feminist politics, preclude a radical enquiry into the political construction and regulation of identity itself?' (Butler, 1990: ix).

Rich was, in fact, self-awarely experiencing more and more difficulty in holding together the notion of a 'common woman' in her deepening understanding of the radical complexities of class, race and lesbian existence. The notion of the lesbian continuum gradually fades out of the picture, in her continuing radical enquiry into the political construction and regulation of identity. Such limiting 'identity' politics can no longer uphold the vision of this major poet and theorist. The next chapter picks up on the further complexities of the notion of 'identity', seeing identity as a field which is multiply configured, fluid, temporary – in continual process, this field is internally and externally contradictory and cannot be fixed into a category. Refusing the universal and transhistoricizing impulse upheld in the terms 'woman' and 'lesbian', Rich returns to the material, to a focus on geographical and historical 'location' in order to bring feminist theory back down to earth again.

Notes

1 I tend to prefer the older term 'woman-identified woman', as it seems to me to gesture towards the idea of an inclusive woman-bonding continuum, leaves room for differences between women to be aired and does not make too many presumptions.

2 Barbara Smith (1977) 'Toward a Black Feminist Criticism', *Conditions: Two*, 1 (2) and in *Conditions: Five: The Black Women's issue*. This article is also anthologised in Showalter (1985: 165–85). The quotation is from Showalter (1985: 170, 172).

5 Back to the Body, Back to Earth

Concrete Experience as 'The Core of Revolutionary Process'

---

the woman trying to fit racism and class into a strictly radical-feminist analysis finds that the box won't pack. The woman who seeks the experiential grounding of identity politics realises that as Jew, white, woman, lesbian, middle-class, she herself has a complex identity.

Adrienne Rich (*BBP*: xii)

I have been working to change the way I speak and write, to incorporate in the manner of telling a sense of place, of not just who I am in the present but where I am coming from, the multiple voices within me. I have confronted silence, inarticulateness. When I say, then, that these words emerge from suffering, I refer to that personal struggle to name that location from which I come to voice – that space of my theorizing.

bell hooks (1991: 146)

This chapter considers the need to locate a feminist politics in time and space, in the experience of the body. Moving away from radical feminism, Rich tentatively formulates a politics of location. She calls for women to resist the urge to theoretical abstraction and urges activist women to again become self-consciously historical-materialist. In this strategic move, the concept of positionality becomes crucial. She seeks to rescue personal experience from its impasse within deconstructivist theory, and also condemns the 'practical dead-endedness' of the exploration of personal experience 'within the proliferation of therapeutic and twelve-step groups'.[1] Personal experience, personal accountability and political responsibility all involve an active engagement with issues, a grounded politics and serious ethical questioning of priorities. Theory must, she believes, again become grounded in the materiality of people's lives. The category of experience has, of course, come under fire within theory, but I suggest in what follows that Rich is very aware that the words themselves have a history, and that they also interpret history: they are indeed, in Joan Scott's words, 'the site of history's enactment' (Scott, 1992: 34).

In opposing current trends in theory, Rich grounds her thinking far less in recent academic theorising than in 'older ideas about economic and social justice, and power'.[2] The move into this new curve of her thinking is documented in '"Going There" and Being Here' (1983). In July 1983 Rich was to attend a conference in Managua, Nicaragua, during the political ferment of the Sandinista revolution. At the conference, Rich met with Latin American writers and intellectuals Claribel Alegría, Julio Cortázar and Ernesto Cardenal, and a wide range of activists from the US, who opposed the US government's intervention in Central American politics.[3] 'While there,' Rich notes:

> I went through moments of feeling contradictions – both within feminism and within the Sandinista revolution – like a physical pain: not just the sensation of being torn apart, but also of long-severed pieces wrenching back together . . . (*BBP*: 156)

Of this conference, Rich comments that: 'Listening to and learning from the women and men dedicated to creating a new Nicaraguan society felt more urgent, more necessary to my own feminist politics than pressing questions like abortion' (ibid.: 157). Turning away strongly from the radical feminism of her earlier thought, she now commits to a new set of political priorities – for, in the urgencies of a society 'born in poverty, menaced from without, the priority at this moment is life itself'. She was to recognise most fundamentally that basic nutrition, illiteracy, and empowerment of the most powerless are also basic women's issues. The frustration and disillusionment she had earlier (and rightly) felt about the 'false integration' of women with the Marxist-influenced New Left, now gives way to a recognition of the necessity to 'keep defining and describing our relationship both to capitalism and to socialism, and to talk seriously about our place in the interconnecting movements for bread, self-determination, dignity, and justice' (ibid.: 159). A profound commitment to concrete experience; to finding ways not only for Central American women but for all women 'to name their own priorities as women'; and to a wider-ranging politics now informs Rich's evolving poetic and theoretical consciousness.

Bringing theory back to earth

Rich signals her growing 'discontent with the polarising impulses within radical feminism' in the foreword to *Blood, Bread and Poetry*. A single identity can no longer be considered a unifying rallying point for political organisation. Rather, a network of intersecting identities 'experienced simultaneously' can be said to constitute Rich's position, for there exists a multiple field of identificatory possibilities within which to move and be moved (*BBP*: 218).[4] Being 'lesbian' can no longer sum up what 'I' am, or 'she' is – for identity is plural, multiply configured, relative, fluid, circumstantial, temporary. The questioning of the validity of any kind of universal or transhistorical identity such as 'lesbian', or 'woman', and of course 'man', both within feminist deconstruction and within the writings of women of colour, begins to give rise to a new and different treatment of 'identity' within Rich's work. Seeing the 'core of revolutionary process' as 'the long struggle against lofty and privileged abstraction', Rich urges a close focus on materiality, on geographical location and voice, which is most fully articulated in 'Notes Toward a Politics of Location' (*BBP*: 213). She stresses these imperatives – 'I need to understand how a place on the map is also a place in history' – and asserts strongly the further need to place the historical and social moment: the context, the precise location in time and space, the 'geography' of a particular statement, the 'When, where, and under what conditions has the statement been true?' (ibid.: 212, 214). But above all, she reaffirms the need to begin with 'the geography closest in – the body' and in so doing, Rich works out her strategy to bring feminist theory 'back down to earth again' (ibid.: 212, 219).

> Theory – the seeing of patterns, showing the forest as well as the trees – theory can be a dew that rises from the earth and collects in the rain cloud and returns to earth over and over. But if it doesn't smell of the earth, it isn't good for the earth. (*BBP*: 213–14)

In putting her case for a focus on material bodily difference, Rich subtly returns to Lacan's hardly earthy formula for understanding sexual difference, in theorising her politics of location. She expands on her earlier attempts to counter the dominance of the phallus through an emphasis on the sexual specificities of the female, but now highlights race as equally important in the construction of identity.[5] Possessing Black or white skin colour assigns 'my body' to a particular social status and position within the specific cultural hierarchy (North American) operating in a specific locality (Baltimore). Just as in Lacan, this designation begins in infancy:

> Even to begin with my body I have to say that from the outset that body had more than one identity. When I was carried out of the hospital into the world, I was viewed and treated as female, but also viewed and treated as white – by both Black and white people. I was located by color and sex as surely as a Black child was located by color and sex – though the implications of white identity were mystified by the presumption that white people are the center of the universe.
>
> To locate myself in my body means more than understanding what it has meant to me to have a vulva and clitoris and uterus and breasts. It means recognising this white skin, the places it has taken me, the places it has not let me go. (*BBP*: 215–16)

However, not like Lacan, this is accessibly written, Rich's language refuses the temptation to soar skywards into elevated theoretical abstraction. Despite her apparent simplicity of presentation and a probably deliberate absence of direct reference, Rich is, I have consistently found, vibrantly alive to the urgencies of feminist 'theory', and is always well informed of its nuances and ramifications. In this passage, with its silent, unreferenced echo of Lacanian theory, possessing whiteness and possessing the phallus

are directly comparable in the sense that they have been desig-
nated a superior position at the centre of the regulatory practices of
North American culture. And so, though it is necessary, it is *not
enough* for feminist theory merely to recognise and affirm the
specificities of the femaleness of the body as a countering strategy – skin colour, racial background, cultural and other locational
differences all matter, in that they function to differentiate one
body from another and to organise, more or less forcefully, *diverse
bodies* towards serving the powerful imperatives of imperialism,
post-colonialism, and white male dominance in whatever form it
manifests itself. Or in other terms: heterosexism, anti-Semitism,
the Christian Right or the major ambience of any other conventional or hegemonic institution.

The poem 'The Spirit of Place', marks the founding moment of
the curve into this new political trajectory (*FDF*: 297–303). In
'knowing how the single-minded, pure / solutions bleached and
desiccated / within their perfect flasks', Rich pursues her growing
sense that, to do justice to 'radical complexity', she must become
'consciously historical': she will uphold 'memory and connectedness, against amnesia and nostalgia' (*BBP*: 145). This cultural
orientation is first indicated in the earlier essay 'Resisting Amnesia:
History and Personal Life' (1983), where she strongly reasserts the
individual and collective responsibility for a full connection to history, materiality and the body.

Identity as field: multiple, layered, complex – and historical

Rich's multiple and overlapping identities offer many points of
departure from now on: not one specific history of oppression
and resistance, but several. Not one, simple, single-minded, politically correct righteousness (was Rich ever guilty of that? surely
not . . .), but a nuanced consciousness of implication in the guilt of
the white dominators. Very much aware of the privilege of whiteness, of middle-classness, of US citizenship – as well as of her
more marginal identities as Jew, lesbian, woman – Rich possesses
not one consciousness but a contingent and revisable multiplicity

of experiencing from different perspectives, each layering the others with further complexity. Identity is thus both continuous and contradictory, composed of, in Audre Lorde's words, 'many different ingredients . . . I find I am constantly being encouraged to pluck out some one aspect of myself and present this as the meaningful whole, eclipsing or denying the other parts of self. But this is a destructive and fragmenting way to live' (Lorde, 1984: 120). Lorde continually challenges Rich, as Rich does Lorde, to rethink and rearticulate her position. As a result of the intense engagement between these two lesbian poets, a heightened aware- ness of the role of innocence and ignorance in consciously or unconsciously reproducing chauvinisms of class, race, religion, heterosexuality, ability and the rest, permeates both Rich's prose and poetry of this period. For example, in the poem 'Virginia 1906', Rich identifies the innocence and the culpability of the white southern woman as a part of her own locational and familial his- tory, and recognises that

This woman I have been and recognize
must know that beneath the quilt of whiteness lies
a hated nation, hers,
earth whose wet places call to mind
still open wounds: her country.
Do we love purity?   Where do we turn for power?

Knowing us as I do I cringe when she says
But I was not culpable,
I was the victim, the girl, the youngest
the susceptible one, I was sick,
the one who simply had to get out, and did
: I am still trying how to think of her power. (*YNL*: 41–2)

The cringe, however, can only come with hindsight, with recog- nitions impossible to make from that place of girl-youth, the place of pure (political) innocence here likened to sickness, from the place of the unaware victim – whose main urgency must be, has to be, a preoccupation with self-preservation, survival, escape from the bonds of convention. The loss of innocence, of youthful unquestioning girlhood, thus has to be conceived of as a complex political / educational process – the maturational process of coming to an informed political position and developing a responsible awareness of collective culpability. Hence the white girl-child's power as oppressor must be weighed against her helpless inno-cence, for acquiring the complex adult-developed political understandings and the refracting distance of a mature under-standing of politics can only come with the poet's commitment to analyse and weigh the micropolitics of each situation – which is, of course, the process of Rich's poems and essays as they are written over time. In the complex analysis of 'Disloyal to Civilisation: Feminism, Racism, Gynephobia' (1978), Rich examines female racism in order to identify the difference between 'actual guilt – or accountability – and guilt feelings' to assess how far it is valid for white women to blame themselves (*LSS*: 281). For 'true' account-ability involves serious ethical questioning, a careful analysis of power relations and an astute, politically and therapeutically aware assessment of responsibility. The poet asks: 'What has she smelled of power without once / tasting it in the mouth?' Some of the radical complexity of this task comes through in the poem: Rich imagines this white woman as possibly having been sexually abused by a white 'Dixie boy' and recognises her refusal to see as a way of keeping herself safe from further violation by creating a wall of innocence around her:

> What if at five years old
> she was old to his fingers splaying her vulva open
> what if forever after, in every record
> she wants her name inscribed as *innocent*

> and will not speak, refuses to know, can say
> *I have been numb for years*
> does not want to hear of any violation
> like or unlike her own, as if the victim
> can be innocent only in isolation
> as if the victim dare not be intelligent

Projection, denial, splitting, forgetting, rationalising, numbing out – the myriad ways we can prevent ourselves from being in touch with what has harmed us. We in our turn need to be aware of our potential for causing further harm: if we are not aware of how we are split, not aware of how we may have incorporated or inter-nalised our abusers, then we ourselves may unconsciously reenact and thus perpetuate abuses we have suffered. (And the 'we' here extends to all humanity.) Rich's engagement with the Otherness (and her identification of the likeness to herself) of this southern white woman does come close to the work of the therapist or analyst, so I offer no apologies for switching to the different language of therapy. Here's Rich: 'My hope is that the movement we are building can further the conscious work of turning Otherness into a keen lens of empathy, that we can bring into being a politics based on concrete, heartfelt understanding of what it means to be Other' (*BBP*: 203).

Staying close to concrete experience

The naming of personal experience as a keystone of radical feminist theory, and the radical feminist position Rich has sometimes struggled to maintain through more than a decade of writing, have, through these exchanges with Black feminist thought, transformed themselves into a new politics. It is helpful to think of this as a newly racially and culturally aware reconfiguration of stances already familiar to her readers, involving a deepening involvement with Jewishness, and an inclusive expansion into a more global feminism – rather than an abandonment of past positions. Crucially, she continues to affirm a commitment to 'staying close to concrete experience':

> Trying to construct ideas and images afresh, by staying close to concrete experience, for the purpose of alleviating a common reality that is felt to be intolerable – this seems to me fair work for the imagination. (*BBP*: xi)

In this characteristic double move, Rich manages to reclaim the historical dimension of personal experience from its theoretical impasse within structuralist theory, and to claim the poet's privilege to speak imaginatively of a 'common reality', that henceforth will not be restricted to a narrow radical feminist focus on 'women': 'Feminist history is not history about women only; it looks afresh at what men have done and how they have behaved, not only toward women but toward each other and the natural world. But the central perspective and preoccupation is *female*, and this implies a vast shift in values and priorities' (*BBP*: 146). The linking of experience with theory and poetry remains key: sex, race, and class 'converge as points of exploitation, there is no "primary oppression" or "contradiction", and it is not patriarchy alone that must be comprehended and dismantled'. (ibid.: xii). The conceptualisations of radical feminism, as of vulgar or academic Marxism, are too simple, and need to be made historically and geographically specific: a new attention to 'the geography I see, lying half in shadow, waiting to be mapped and recorded', which was first signalled in the foreword to 'Disloyal to Civilisation', comes increasingly to the fore (*LSS*: 275).

Politically, the hope that runs through *A Wild Patience Has Taken Me This Far* is that the necessary focus may be created through a feminism, 'which looks with fresh eyes on all that has been trivialised, devalued, forbidden, or silenced in female history' (*LSS*: 263):

> past and present   near and far
> the Alabama quilt
> the Botswana basket
> history   the dark crumble
>
> of last year's compost
> filtering softly through your living hand (*FDF*: 299)

The flesh, the body, 'your living hand' are inextricably part of the makings of history, bound up with it, inseparable from it. My body, yours too, 'cannot help making history because we are made of it, and history is made of people like us, carriers of the behaviour and assumptions of a given time and place' (*BBP*: 144). And so the word 'history' takes on new culturally specific meaning here as 'we search with awe and pride into the flare and authority of women's imaginations translated into quilts, and study the histories secreted in colors, stitches, materials' (ibid.: 151). In eschewing the narrower focus of the radical feminist mode she had adopted throughout the seventies, Rich reaffirms here a more complicated, unsentimental, materialist commitment to history and to our location on the earth 'our / world as it is if not as it might be / then as it is – in its full range and depth of political imperative (*FDF*: 302).

Always acutely aware of the workings of power, in honouring

history and its legacy in the present, Rich addresses the needs, problems, urgencies of the powerless in particular specific geographical and temporal locations. She locates where responsibility lies and highlights the crucial political strategy of 'feeding the hungry so that they have the energy to think about what they want beyond food' (*BBP*: 158). The notion of positionality, or of identity as not only constructed from within but also produced by and within and through the socio-political matrix – as shaped that is, by forces outside the individual subject – in a simultaneity of oppressions, becomes extended to include fundamental questions regarding 'literacy, infant mortality, the fundamental issue of having something to eat' (ibid.: 163). The concept of positionality in Rich's thought, despite its acceptance of a multiple and contradictory identity, nonetheless does not abandon the agential mode of assigning responsibility and urging political action.

However, in theorising the multiplicity of relations of subordination within a radical democratic politics, feminists must not abandon the feeling, passionate, pain-bearing, damaged, desiring body, in a world in which pain is 'meant to be gagged / uncured ungrieved-over:

> The problem is
> to connect, without hysteria, the pain
> of any one's body with the pain of the body's world
> For it is the body's world
> they are trying to destroy forever
> The best world is the body's world
> filled with creatures   filled with dread
> misshapen so   yet the best we have
> our raft among the abstract worlds (*YNL*: 100)

Rich rarely mentions her long relationship with rheumatoid arthritis, a disability for which she has had many operations. Surprisingly, there are relatively few poems that highlight disability as a political issue. In this poem, structural symmetry and the 'logic of limits, margins, borders and boundaries' between language and the body-in-pain is turned inside out: 'I feel signified by pain / from my breastbone through my left shoulder down / through my elbow into my wrist is a thread of pain' (ibid.: 89). Diana Fuss has suggested that

Inside/outside functions as the very figure for signification and the mechanisms of meaning production. It has everything to do with the structures of alienation, splitting, and identification which together produce a self and an other, a subject and an object, an unconscious and a conscious, an interiority and an exteriority. (Fuss, 1991: 1)

Those hampered in their bodies have long been alienated from 'the mechanisms of meaning production' that would identify and meet their needs, in that many buildings are clearly not designed to accommodate wheelchairs, to provide good light conditions, good acoustics. Consideration of specific special needs must still be fought for, and, even where budgetary allocation is provided, this needs to be at the inception of projects rather than as an afterthought. All these difficulties are an outcome of this splitting, as a manifest failure to imagine the other person or group in the fullness of their existence. Being abandoned to an outside by those 'in charge of definitions' certainly builds feelings of individual frustration towards those who have the power to implement changes and who yet remain impervious to the other's suffering body:

> if my fury at being grounded frightens you
> take off on your racing skis
> in your beautiful tinted masks
> Trapped in one idea, you can't have feelings
> Without feelings perhaps you can feel like a god. (*YNL*: 101)

The world of abstraction, as of theory, is again fiercely brought to task for failing to be grounded in concrete experience. Any politics that is 'cut off from the ongoing lives of women or of men, rarefied into an elite jargon', will lead to the frustration and defeat of a 'dead end' (*BBP*: 217).

History, desire and the creative process

> I have seen a woman sitting
> between the stove and the stars
> her fingers singed from snuffing out the candles
> of pure theory   Finger and thumb: both scorched:
> I have felt that sacred wax blister my hand (*TP*: 45)

Over time, Rich's challenging ideas have provided a stimulus to theory and an ongoing critique both of theory and political practice. In the maturity of her thought, Rich returns and returns to her earlier work – a nip here, a tuck there – to question earlier certainties, to review, to revise. During a visit to the UK in 1994, Rich is quoted as saying 'We get so much better as we get older. You get clearer, your priorities are more distinct. You give up certain kinds of vanity, which is very freeing' (Birkett, 1994: 11). The older and clearer Rich, who has long watched, participated in and criticised the transformations of feminist movements in North America, is especially critical of recent feminist excursions into the related (male-dominated) fields of post-structuralist and/or post-Lacanian theory: 'Since the seventies there has been an emergence of so-called feminist literary theory – very elite, drawing on language that most women would not read' (Birkett, 1994: 11). These 'elite' languages have become predominant in many educational institutions in both the US and the UK. Many students find themselves necessarily engaging with theory in order to survive academia and emerge with the trophy of a degree. I have attempted in this book to recognise this as a fact of life, while at the same time I have sought to be true to the spirit of Rich's work.

In the eighties and nineties, following her trip to Nicaragua in 1983, Rich re-engages with the more Marxist feminist perspectives of Central American liberation movements, and particularly those of women of colour:

> I want to suggest that United States feminism has a peculiar potential to break out of the nightmare and place itself more intelligently with other liberation movements (often led by women from whom we have much to learn) because the spiritual and moral vision of the United States women's movement is increasingly being shaped by women of color. The concepts of identity politics, of simultaneity of oppressions, of concrete experience as the touchstone for ideology, the refusal to accept "a room of one's own" in exchange for not threatening the system – these have been explored, expanded on, given voice most articulately by women of color . . . (*BBP*: 165)

Given the political and theoretical context in which her work was produced and which permeates both Rich's poetry and prose, this strong movement towards an anti-deconstruction, anti-academic stance merits further consideration. Elizabeth Meese, in her essay 'Re-Figuring Feminist Criticism', has identified 'the threat of a feminism which, figuring itself in its own voice from the site of the academy, fails to engage the political conditions of women who speak and write from other locations and other voices'. She warns of 'the perilous risks' we run if we are not aware of the effects of differences within feminist theory: 'the most worrisome being persistent fragmentation and alienation which undermine feminism's ability to form coalitions needed to bring about change (even on the level of the academic institution)' (Meese, 1990: 4). These concerns fuel the urgency of Rich's desire to find an 'impetus to action', to be accessible and to maintain a political edge, and propel her towards embracing the work of women of colour – publicly rejecting the elite languages of discourse theory. Theory, of course, informs the deep structure of lesbian identity politics, and also provides the rationale for articulating a politics of the dispossessed, the marginal, the 'other' – ideas utterly foundational to Rich's later thought. But though aware of academic theoretical issues, her commitment to an older politics of social justice and economic power profoundly informs her thinking. This contradictory position may create difficulty for those reliant on current theorising to give them a way of approaching her writing, but at the same time her statement alerts critics to the necessity to create a socially effective, accountable and politically responsible literary criticism capable of addressing the global concerns of her more recent work.

Rich has herself over the years made crucially important contributions to thinking about desire, language and cultural critique, as well as bodying forth her powerful critique of theoretical abstraction. She has also committed herself to a renewed political engagement with materiality, history and experience: 'I am pursued by questions of historical process, of historical responsibility, questions of historical consciousness and ignorance and what these have to do with power' (*BBP*: 137). Again, in *What is Found There*, her most recent book of prose writings, Rich calls for a renewed focus on history and experience as a way forward into the future for the politically aware. The book 'reflects' the undertaking

> by one kind of artist, to see and feel her way to an understanding of her art's responsive and responsible relationship to history, to her contemporaries, and to the future. I have never believed that poetry is an

escape from history, and I do not think it is more, or less, necessary than food, shelter, health, education, decent working conditions. It is as necessary. (*WIFT*: xiv)

To reclaim history, the concrete and particular as well as the collective experiences energising the 'freedom movements fermenting around the world in this late twentieth century', as I have argued, seems to require Rich to reject 'theory' (*BBP*: 166). The authority of experience, the claim of 'history' is that it apparently offers valid documentary evidence of causes for concern – it illuminates lives lived, shapes identities formed in resistance, and gives the lie to dominant viewpoints: it can point to alternative ways of viewing the world. The difficulty is – and no one is more aware of this than Rich herself – that, as Scott suggests, 'questions about the constructed nature of experience, about how subjects are constituted as different in the first place, about how one's vision is structured – about language (or discourse) and history – are left aside' (Scott, 1992: 25).

Claims to identity and difference are deeply bound up with the narratives, stories, documentaries, histories and poems coming out of experience – and yet the appeal to 'experience' too often 'precludes critical examination of the workings of the ideological system itself' (ibid.: 24–5). As Joan W. Scott has argued: 'what could be truer, after all, than a subject's own account of what he or she has lived through? It is precisely this kind of appeal to experience as incontestable evidence and as an originary point of explanation – as a foundation upon which analysis is based – that weakens the critical thrust of histories of difference.'

But Rich, very much concerned with holding up to question falsely framed choices, is less than convinced that the appeal to history, the authority of experience, the incontestable documentary fact – the empiricist historicism that has underpinned much of US women's studies – can be relied on as a foundational concept to approach her own writing as a feminist and poet, even though she is strongly drawn to the politics of historical materialism. She reminds us of Muriel Rukeyser's line:

'Breathe in experience, breathe out poetry.' There is a sense of transmutation: something has to happen between the breathing in of experience and the breathing out of poetry. It has been transformed, not only into words but into something new. (*ARP*: 253)

Language has long been a site of struggle within her work, but here she comments specifically on the tension between seeing poetry 'as a sort of documentation of the poet's life, as perhaps a kind of autobiography' and 'seeing poetry as unrelated to life and history and social circumstances'. In reading poetry, as with reading any kind of writing whatever, there is a need to be aware of the fact of ideological construction. But a poem is, in Rich's terms, 'a construction of language that uses, tries to use everything that language can do, to conjure, to summon up something that's not quite knowable in any other way. Using the tonal and musical aspects of language, the image-making aspect of language, the associations between words, the merging aspect of language in metaphor where one thing can actually become another and throw light on both' (*ARP*: 254).

It is easy to overread in terms of the biographical in relation to Rich's writings, given the acting out of her feminist commitment to 'the personal is political' within her writings. Indeed, her politically (and personally) motivated necessity to identify the 'splits', the multiplicity and diversity of her own 'sources', has led me in turn to take the risk of autobiographical overreading in charting the major shifts in Rich's ideas over time. But I hope that in doing so I have not lost sight of the discursive nature of 'experience' as a construction within language. I have sought 'to understand the operations of the complex and changing discursive processes by which identities are ascribed, resisted, or embraced' in my chartings of the complexities of Rich's constantly changing self-identifications – just as I have taken the 'emergence of concepts and identities as historical events in need of an explanation' (Scott, 1992: 33). As Joan W. Scott stresses:

Subjects are constituted discursively, experience is a linguistic event (it doesn't happen outside established meanings) but neither is it confined to a fixed order of meaning. Since discourse is by definition shared, experience is collective as well as individual. Experience is a subject's history. Language is the site of history's enactment. Historical explanation cannot, therefore, separate the two. (ibid.: 34)

Experience is a linguistic event, experience is a subject's history, language is the site of history's enactment – I make no apologies for underlining here Scott's words, for theory in its turn has excluded a whole dimension of analysis that has cried out for critical attention to be brought to bear on it. For theory too brings in its trail many related and complex issues. Breaking through the borders and boundaries of even feminist thought Rich, in the poem 'North American Time', takes on the vexed question of 'lived experience', as of 'the working history of the words themselves' (*YNL*: 33; *WIFT*: 86–8). In her terms, it is the use to which the words are put that is more important than the space and time and moment of their writing. No one is more aware that, whatever the intention motivating the writing, the words themselves become independent of the writer, become active in their own right, create their own history, once out in the world, for if 'Language is the site of history's enactment', then layer on layer of contesting interpretations provide further 'evidence' of histories' enactments. And poetry becomes part of that history in which language participates – as another 'experience'. As a linguistic event, it is historical to its core:

> Poetry never stood a chance
> of standing outside history.
> One line typed twenty years ago
> can be blazed on a wall in spraypaint
> to glorify art as detachment . . .

> We move   but our words stand
> become responsible
> for more than we intended (*YNL*: 33)

In these few lines Rich puts into clear perspective the difficulties of assuming a direct relationship between the art of writing and 'lived experience'. Here, she identifies the temporal, spatial and appropriative distortions that create distance rather than closeness between the work of the writer and the readers who will interpret the words she writes. For language can be appropriated, bent to a new purpose, interpreted in ways undreamt of by the poet: 'words – / whether we like it or not – / stand in a time of their own' (*YNL*: 35). Words lose their historical context with the passage of time, they may be reinscribed in countless ways – sympathetically or derisively – by poets, critics, students, biographers and the rest. The author herself, however powerful an inscriber of her own meanings, cannot foresee the history of her words once they are published, for they are out of her control, and will constantly be under threat of mis- or reinterpretation.

Rich's work overall adds a further dimension to these complexities around historical 'truth', by accepting and including the 'truths' of the unconscious made available in and through dreams and images – an aspect frequently left out of account by theorists, sometimes even those most deeply influenced by psychoanalytic insights. Rich has throughout her work in both theory and poetry recognised the importance of dreamwork in forming her deepest insights, her poetry, her political perspectives.

In the course of this book, I have sought to show this strategy in action – the interweaving of documentary fact with the 'truths' of dreams, desires, sexualities and subjectivities – so characteristic of Rich's work in both prose and poetry. In *Of Woman Born*, for example, personal testimony is set alongside documentary reportage: speculation, analysis and theory interrelate with image, fantasy and myth. And the power and energy of her poetic voice resonates throughout her prose writings, even where she is passionately arguing hard politics. For her, it is as important to examine the individual dream life as it is to address the politics, for even the dream life is situated within and emerges out of unconscious experience which, of course, also has a history. Inescapably personal but also political, dreams are bound to their historical moment of production. Being endlessly subject to reinterpretation, they are themselves an interpretation. Rich calls here for the necessity to be vigilant, to be aware that limits, boundaries, borders – whether to feminist theory, to politics, to poetry or to dream – can operate even at this deepest, image-making level of the psyche:

> When my dreams showed signs
> of becoming
> politically correct
> no unruly images
> escaping beyond borders
> when walking in the street I found my

themes cut out for me
knew what I would not report
for fear of enemies' usage
then I began to wonder. (*YNL*: 33)

Accountability, responsibility – asking these profound questions – 'What is missing here? how am I using this? – becomes part
of the creative process' (Montenegro, 1991: 260). I agree with Rich
when she claims that 'poetry can break open locked chambers of
possibility, restore numbed zones to feeling, recharge desire'
(*WIFT*: xiv). If desire itself becomes boundaried within the systems and coercions of corporate capitalism, our power to imagine
becomes stultified. If the poet's 'themes' are delimited through the
fear of 'enemies' usage', and even her role as witness is inhibited
through fear of comebacks, then the vital role of the revolutionary
writer to know words, to use words, to rely on words to imagine
and to convey the necessity to create a just, humane society, may
be undermined. As Rich has suggested, 'the wick of desire' always
projects itself towards a possible future – and, in this revolutionary
art, becomes 'an alchemy through which waste, greed, brutality,
frozen indifference, "blind sorrow" and anger are transmuted into
some drenching recognition of the *what if?* – the possible' (*WIFT*:
241). However, the knowledge that comes from our embodied experience is, in Rich's work, inextricable from the languages in which it
is spoken, thought, imaged, dreamed. It is a theme which recurs
throughout Rich's work to date: our concrete needs, the passionate
urgency of our desires, the intensity of women's diverse struggles –
these are identified and identifiable, just as our differences can be
identified and are identifiable as continually in process and are
always to be held up to question.

Taking nothing for granted, maintaining a continual vigilance
against taking anything presumed to be 'true' at its face value,
Rich constantly questions the premises of her own thought, working critically with the language she uses. If 'language is the site of
history's enactment', then it is also for Rich the site for questioning
that history of experience; for evaluating the impositions and alien-
ations that are the outcome of domination; for plumbing the depths
and analysing the complexities of what constitutes identity. For
over 40 years, Rich has found herself interpreting and reinterpreting

the contradictory social realities of women's lives, always critically conscious of the workings of power – not only 'possessive, exploitative power' but also 'the power to engender, to create, to bring forth fuller life' (*WIFT*: 49). These are large aims, befitting the work of this major feminist theorist and revolutionary poet.

In the chapter that follows, I trace Rich's return to sources: her examination of the anti-Semitism in her own family and her reclamation of her inheritance as a Jew. In her thought, the very meaning of 'home' moves out from the centre to embrace the margin and again, as so often, she calls into question her own presuppositions, engaging once more with otherness – the otherness of maleness, of the history of the persecution of the Jews – in this even wider formulation of her holistic, ecosensitive global politics.

Notes

1 On reading this manuscript, Rich noted that 'I felt the need not only to "rescue personal experience from its impasse within deconstructivist theory," but also from its practical dead-endedness within the proliferation of therapeutic and twelve-step groups.' In my turn, responding to Rich, I want to say that I consider 12-step groups to be often rigid, dogmatic and not always very helpful to a person in recovery. I nonetheless believe that group therapy, and individual therapy, play an essential role in enabling recovery from all forms of abuse – racial, sexual, emotional, physical – and do have the valuable function of interrupting the cycle of oppression. I suggest that the changes achieved through therapy in one person's life have the potential to effect change in many lives. One individual who becomes able to 'cut through the crap' within their family or work environment, changes that family or that workplace. Another person may relate differently to his/her children and so may effect change in the next generation. Therapy can thus be seen as just another way of being political. It can also be a valuable resource when burnout threatens, or when resignation saps political energy. But the point I am trying to make is that it is the way individual and group therapy is used, rather than therapy as such, that needs further attention. Rich's point may have more to do with time-consuming self-preoccupation at the expense of activism, but I would argue that for many women activism would be impossible without therapy that enables them to heal from their injuries within. It is true that the UK's deep resistance to things therapeutic creates a very different picture for me, and I acknowledge that my comments here do not necessarily illuminate the US context, nor do they attempt to address the wider issues of economic misery, the acceleration of corporate power and Christian extremism; and they do not take away the necessity for urgent political action in the struggle to achieve social justice for all.

2 Rich's notes to this MS.

3 Ibid. This movement, though much smaller than the Vietnam movement of the sixties and seventies, raised aid for people's movements in El Salvador, Guatemala, Cuba and Nicaragua, and exposed CIA terrorism against such movements.

4 Rich quotes from the 1977 Combahee River Collective statement, 'a major document of the US women's movement, which gives a clear and uncompromising Black-feminist naming to the experience of simultaneity of oppressions'.

5 See Lacan's 'twin doors', one labelled Ladies, the other Gentlemen, as an illustration of 'the laws of urinary segregation'. Jaques Lacan, 'The Agency of the Letter in the Unconscious or Reason since Freud', in Lacan (1977: 151). See also Jacqueline Rose's theoretical elaboration and critique of Lacan. This further account of how anatomical difference – having or not having the phallus – 'comes to figure sexual difference, that is, it becomes the sole representative of what that difference is allowed to be', is a foundational (white) feminist articulation of the way gender difference becomes inscribed in cultural forms. This astute contestation of Lacan's formulation, in centring itself around the critique of the notion of having or not having the phallus 'as a reduction of difference to an instance of visible perception', itself takes no account of race as another crucially significant difference (Mitchell and Rose, 1982: 42).

6 Inside and Outside, Centre and Margin, Jew and Gentile

the Contradictory World of Multiple, Threshold Identity

Split at the root, neither Gentile nor Jew
Yankee nor Rebel, born
in the face of two ancient cults,
I'm a good reader of histories . . .

Adrienne Rich[1]

I had no choice. I had to struggle and resist to emerge from that
context and then from other locations with mind intact, with an
open heart. I had to leave that space I called home to move
beyond boundaries, yet I needed also to return there . . .

bell hooks[2]

The Black experience of colonised (and enslaved) otherness lends a
profound complexity to Rich's theorising of the frontiers of difference. It is perceivable in her thought as a tangible honing of a political
edge that begins in the early eighties to turn much more strongly to
address other kinds of personally and globally experienced outsiderhood and invisibility. It surfaces most emphatically in those poems
that explore her own otherness – her disabilities, her Jewishness, her

lesbianism – but also in those which extend to include queer, Black, Puerto Rican, Chicana, Native American and the many 'others' marginalised within the dominant white culture. And, just as the notion of 'coming out' cannot be limited to sexual preference, so being an outsider or taking the chance to speak from a marginal position cannot be limited to radical feminism. The return to roots, the attempt to reconnect to sources, to reconsider what meaning 'home' has for her – already strong themes within Black feminist writings – become imperatives within Rich's work and provide a focus for this rather more biographically oriented chapter. Subtly, Rich begins to grapple with the profound theoretical complexity of a contradictory and unfixed self-positioning, multiply located in time and space, in speaking from within her own experience. I would also suggest, that in this struggle for clarity Rich is clearly influenced by Anzaldúa's troubled question: 'Who are my people?' in making this attempt to locate herself politically and spiritually:

> I am a wind-swayed bridge, a crossroads inhabited by whirlwinds. Gloria, the facilitator. Gloria the mediator, straddling the walls between abysses. 'Your allegiance is to La Raza, the Chicano movement,' say the members of my race. 'Your allegiance is to the Third World,' say my Black and Asian friends. 'Your allegiance is to your gender, to women,' say the feminists. Then there's my allegiance to the Gay movement, to the socialist revolution, to the New Age, to magic and the occult. And there's my affinity to literature, to the world of the artist. What am I? *A third world lesbian feminist with Marxist and mystic leanings.* They would chop me up into little fragments and tag each piece with a label. (Anzaldúa, 1983: 205)

So too, Rich examines her own allegiances to Jewish, Black, gay and feminist cultures during the mid- to late eighties, and early nineties. She refuses identification with any form of unitary identity and, eschewing single-issue radical-feminist politics, expansively includes a multiplicity of differences, bringing them into tension and play in the urgently politicised fields of her writings.

The return to roots

This urgency to re-evaluate her position seems as much influenced by Black experience and culture as by the rising influence of an emergent Jewish feminist movement. As Evelyn Torton Beck explains: 'I was pained but not surprised to feel invisible as a lesbian among Jews. I was terribly disappointed and confused to feel invisible as a Jew among lesbians' (Beck, 1982: xviii).[3] The demand for anti-Semitism to be taken seriously in a lesbian-feminist movement already pledged to acknowledge and struggle with diversity and difference has now led to the further challenge: the call for women to examine their conscious and unconscious anti-Semitism in the same way as they are called to examine their racism. It is this imperative that motivates Rich, in what is probably her most autobiographical writing to date, to begin to re-examine the internalised anti-Semitism of her own life and family. In this extract from 'Sources', her thought curves inward, holding to a sense of inner strength – even as she painfully recognises the ways in which the necessity to survive has distorted too many lives and relationships, including those in her own family:

> Everything that has ever
> helped me has come through what already
> lay stored in me   Old things, diffuse, unnamed, lie strong
> across my heart.
>
>   This is from where
> my strength comes, even when I miss my strength
> even when it turns on me
> like a violent master. (*YNL*: 4)

Accessing the multiplicity of 'sources' within the diversity of her own family leads Rich, in the deepest way, to attempt 'to be honest with myself, trying to figure out why writing this seems to be so dangerous an act' (*BBP*: 100; first published in Beck, 1982). White southern (Christian raised) lesbian writer and poet, Minnie Bruce Pratt, in her important essay 'Identity: Skin, Blood, Heart', identifies the fear-filled complexity of seeking to understand her own familial history. On a parallel journey, she too acknowledges her difficult inheritance:

> As I've worked at stripping away layer after layer of my false identity, notions of skin, blood, heart based in racism and anti-Semitism, another way I've tried to regain my self-respect, to keep from feeling completely naked and ashamed of who it is I am, is to look at what I have carried with me from my culture that could help me in the process. As I learned

about the actual history and present of my culture, I didn't stop loving
my family or my home, but it was hard to figure out what from there I
could be proud and grateful to have: since much of what I had learned
had been based on false pride. Yet buried under the layers, I discovered
some strengths. (Bulkin et al., 1984: 43–4)

These urgencies – to explore in a complex act of remembrance
what 'home', parents, her family of origin can now mean for her –
fuel Rich's painful journey of reminiscence: it takes real courage to
make this return to

> the family coil   so twisted, tight and loose
> anyone trying to leave
> has to strafe the field
> burn the premises down (*YNL*: 56)

The 'struggle of memory against forgetting' her contradictory
Jewish inheritance is spelled out in the essay 'Split at the Root: An
Essay on Jewish Identity' (1982) (*BBP*: 100). Rich has confirmed
that she frequently writes her poems out of the same nexus of
concern as her essays: 'A lot of my . . . essays have points of intersection with poems, probably none so much as "Split at the Root"
with "Sources" – which I was writing at about the same time'
(Montenegro, 1991: 267). And this strategy for writing does lend
itself to a consideration of the ways the poem and the essay interrelate. The concept of 'location', in time as in space, makes it
reasonable also to contemplate the further interrelationships
between feminisms and lesbian and gay theories as and when they
throw light on Rich's thought.

Identity and assimilation: claiming a contradictory inheritance . . .

Rich's Jewish identity comes from her father's side, not through
the maternal line. Her father – of mixed Sephardic and Ashkenazic
descent (but brought up to be a white southern gentleman) – was
a Jew with 'no use for organised religion' (*BBP*: 110). Her Gentile
mother was a white southern (social) Christian. Her husband, to
her parents, was 'a Jew of the "wrong kind" from an orthodox
eastern European background'. According to Rich, he was pulled

'toward Yankee approval, assimilation . . . It was as if you could have it both ways – identity and assimilation – without having to think about it very much' (ibid.: 115). As critical of him as of herself, Rich alludes to the necessity felt by many Jews of her own and her parents' generation, following the crisis and dire extremity of the Holocaust, to behave in self-protective ways. As Lucy Dawidowicz had put it, in *The War against the Jews*:

> To facilitate their survival in powerlessness and to lessen the impact of humiliation and suffering, the Jews made virtues of self-discipline, prudence, moderation, forgoing present gratification for eventual benefit. They learned to practise non-violent means of resistance and to find ways of circumventing discrimination and deflecting persecution. (1975: 412)

Exposing assimilation as a self-protective strategy for survival, this 'passing' – utterly necessary in the years following the Holocaust – as leading to loneliness, isolation, cultural alienation, outsiderhood and a false sense of safety, Rich, influenced by Michelle Cliff, and the Jewish women's workshop at Storrs, Connecticut, begins to examine her own 'passing' (*BBP*: 100). Some of the questions to be asked of this identification, whether in prose or in poetry, are voiced here by Beck, in her introduction to the important collection of essays, *Nice Jewish Girls: A Lesbian Anthology*:

> So we ask, collectively, in different voices, genres and styles: What does it mean for us to identify as Jewish lesbians? In what ways have we internalized our Jewishness? How are we, as Jews, different from each other (by place of birth, life history, relationship to tradition, race, class, age), and in what ways are we the same? What sparks of recognition fly between us when we meet as Jewish lesbians? (1982: xxx)

To identify as Jewish for Rich meant that 'I have to be willing to do two things: I have to claim my father for I have my Jewishness from him and not from my gentile mother; and I have to break his silence, his taboos . . . And there is, of course, the third thing: I have to face the sources and the flickering presence of my own ambivalence as a Jew . . .' (*BBP*: 100). I have suggested that to do this will necessitate a return to childhood and to memories of 'home'.

Re-visioning 'home'

The poem, 'In the Wake of Home', identifies the emptinesses, the abandonments, the losses, of that place 'where absence began':

> Any time you go back
> the familiar underpulse
> will start its throbbing: *Home, home!*
> and the hole torn and patched over
> will gape unseen again (*YNL*: 58)

'Family central, home both refuge and locus of pain': there is little comfort in Rich's vision of home in this poem, which expands its concerns to include a notion of home as 'this continent of the homeless', and 'this planet of warworn children / women and children standing in line' (*WIFT*: 23). 'Home', in this inclusive, both/and vision, holds in tension both negative and positive polarity and does not leave out of account the homeless, the abandoned, the hungry. In the poem, then, the romantic nostalgia of the desiring pulse drawing her back is juxtaposed with the necessity to expand the significances carried within the word, Rich's political urgency is to transform its meaning and to throw light on the multiform dimensions of what the notion of 'home' could mean to a global feminism.

In bell hooks's complex Black lesbian feminist perspective, which is clearly influenced by Rich's theorising, 'home' is a key location and yet its significance can be elusive: 'At times, home is nowhere. At times, one knows only extreme estrangement and alienation. Then home is no longer just one place. It is locations.' Thus the location of 'home' can imply a centre – providing love, nourishment, growth, security – or may be a place located at the margins, at an edge where insecurity, deprivation, loss, estrangement are the order of the day. Either, or both at the same time. Children survive, or don't survive; comfort may, or may not, come.

Margin and centre, both/and . . .

For hooks, 'survival depended on an ongoing public awareness of the separation between margin and center – and the private acknowledgement that we were a necessary, vital part of that whole' (hooks 1991: 149). hooks's political agenda undoubtedly required her to locate herself on an exquisite edge: 'We looked both from the outside in and from the inside out. We focused attention on the center as well as on the margin. We understood both' (hooks 1991: 149). Marginality in her thought is, she claims, 'much more than a site of deprivation . . . it is also the site of radical possibility, a space of resistance'. Yet marginality is also 'a site one stays in, clings to even, because it nourishes one's capacity to resist' rather than staying in a place of collective despair, or deprivation, or estrangement (ibid.: 150). On the other hand, to feel part of the whole – of 'the main body' – is to refuse segregation, whether based on gender, religion, race, ability or sexuality. It is profoundly to resist the effects of dispersal and fragmentation of community. Both/and.

For a lesbian renowned for her active resistance to patriarchy, a long-time outsider who has consistently refused to assimilate into either mainstream academia or mainstream American poetry, who has eschewed the approval, even power, that path might have brought her, these are huge challenges. Rich has, over time, seen and spoken from the outside in, critically examining the (white, Christian, able-bodied, heterosexual, powerful male) centre from that marginal position 'outside the law' so intensely that this necessity to return to sources constitutes another radical shift of perspective: she now takes on the task of reassessing her relation to her father and her ex-husband. Breaking down the opposition between margin and centre and moving towards a more holistic, both/and understanding of her Jewish inheritance meant that Rich had to break down even further the dualistic logic which had structured her strategy of resistance. As a white feminist arguing against patriarchy, she found herself yet again calling into question her own presuppositions:

> With the new politics, activism, literature of a tumultuous feminist movement around me, a movement which claimed universality though it had not yet acknowledged its own racial, class and ethnic perspectives, or its fears of the differences among women – I pushed aside for one last time thinking further about myself as a Jewish woman. I saw Judaism simply as yet another strand of patriarchy. If asked to choose I might have said (as my father had said in another language): *I am a woman, not a Jew.* (*BBP*: 122)

Just what is involved in not pushing away, not denying either the southern social Christian or the Jew within? Radical complexity demanded that she examine all aspects to each question, the dual inheritance of her Gentile mother, Jewish father and husband. If the 'centres' of patriarchy – religious, secular, social – were no longer thinkable in monochrome as the overarching oppressor, if radical complexity rather than radical feminism meant anything, it meant that Rich must engage once again with the Otherness of maleness, as of Judaism. She must self-critically explore the gaps, silences, absences, erasures – the 'unadressed places' of her own position (*YRG*: 146).

Hitler's Final Solution: how to engage with that otherness?

She retraces, in 'Split at the Root', her own journey, reclaiming its legacies of suffering and pain, as well as celebrating what was joyful and rich and nourishing within her own life: a task undertaken in order to find ways of illuminating and transforming an emergent, more globally sensitive, political vision. In a sense, in making this return to sources she is living out in activist ways her re-visionary strategy, as well as doing some necessary psychological 'work' towards her own survival in a hostile world. For, in claiming a Jewish identity as a lesbian feminist, she inevitably comes face to face with the sober, essential facts of Hitler's war against the Jewish people, his 'Final Solution of the Jewish Question', and the con-comitant understanding that 'the Holocaust did not transcend history, but was part of the recurrent pattern of persecution that has been the Jewish historical experience' (Dawidowicz, 1975: 20). Her poignant, dry comment – 'According to Nazi logic, my two Jewish grandparents would have made me *a Mischling, first-degree* – non-exempt from the Final Solution' – shows that yes, though she has a deep struggle with herself, she is becoming more able to hear 'the broken voice', 'the speech of suffering' of her people (*BBP*: 103; *YRG*, 146). But, before she can align herself more fully, she must locate herself in relation to both – margin *and* centre – and she must identify what complexities of relation she has to the terrifying

Otherness of this history of persecution, if she wishes to see herself as a part of the (Jewish) whole. The need is to understand both.

Overthrowing the father – and reconsidering patriarchy

Rich speaks of her relation to her father, in an interview with David Montenegro, as an 'extremely adversarial relationship' (1991: 263). In 'After Dark', a poem written in 1964 (two years after Plath's 'Daddy' was published), the process of coming to terms with this powerfully ambiguous, somehow mythic figure has already begun:

> You are falling asleep and I sit looking at you
> old tree of life
> old man whose death I wanted
> I can't stir you up now. (*FDF*: 68)

 Written four years before her father's death in 1968, after a long debilitating illness, this poem grapples with ambivalence, with the complexity of the power struggle between them: the father's indulgent tyranny, the daughter's rebellious love.[4] Yet his failing health, his giving ground, is as difficult for her to cope with as his tyranny: 'When your memory fails – / no more to scourge my inconsistencies – / the sashcords of the world fly loose. / A window crashes / suddenly down'. Rich speaks in 'Split at the Root' of the obsessional power of his voice delivering its critical monologues with 'a driving intensity' which, as in the poem, assumes the right to 'know' the daughter, better than the daughter knows her self: 'His investment in my intellect and talent was egotistical, tyrannical, opinionated, and terribly wearing' (*BBP*: 113). At the same time, this man taught her, within this 'difficult force field', to become a writer – 'to write and rewrite; to feel that I *was* a person of the book, even though a woman; to take ideas seriously . . .' (ibid.).

 Recovering from this overwhelming invasiveness was going to take years. Maybe the sometimes rage-filled urgency fuelling Rich's engagement with feminism finds its own deep source in this primary encounter with a man utterly determined to control and shape his daughter. According to Rich, Arnold Rich was deeply entrenched in denial, locked into a 'private defence system so elaborate' that his daughter must finally ask 'What happens when survival seems to mean closing off one emotional artery after another?' (*BBP*: 114). It is an old, old story, and the anger still burns through of that frustrated child, who must 'overthrow the father, take what he taught her and use it against him' (*YNL*: 9). However, in identifying her father as at the root of her concept of patriarchy, Rich now looks back in her characteristic re-visionary gesture, self-critically reassessing her political position:

> After your death I met you again as the face of patriarchy, could name at last precisely the principle you embodied, there was an ideology at last which let me dispose of you, identify the suffering you caused, hate you righteously as part of a system, the kingdom of the fathers. I saw the power and arrogance of the male as your true watermark; I did not see beneath it the suffering of the Jew, the alien stamp you bore, because you had deliberately arranged that it should be invisible to me. (ibid.: 9)

This important statement marks a breakthrough – yes, to a recognition of the individual male as vulnerable, as having suffered, as merely human; an acceptance too that while the notion of patriarchy may provide a convenient fiction, it is too crude a concept to speak to the Jewish experience. But the statement also marks another beginning theoretically. As writer and as theoretician, she accepts that she too suffers 'lapses in meaning', 'blanks' of denial which interfere with her perceptions – she too shares this history of assimilation, of passing – and yet must still speak (*BBP*: 84). In this speaking, a new principle comes to the fore:

> it is another beginning, for me. Not just a way of saying, in 1982 Right-Wing America, *I too will wear the yellow star*. It's a moving into accountability, enlarging the range of accountability. (ibid.: 123)

Surviving suicide . . . surviving the Holocaust

In the profound poem 'Sources', Rich begins at last to come to terms with this whole difficult issue. There, she breaks through many years of silence in speaking of her husband's suicide: he 'ended isolate, who had tried to move in the floating world of the assimilated who know and deny they will always be aliens. Who drove to Vermont in a rented car at dawn and shot himself' (*YNL*: 19). Something of her anger – 'threaded with love' – comes through in this difficult recognition of his closed-off world, as of the assimilative manoeuvres, the self-destructive strategies he felt compelled to employ. The sense of loss, the sense of the futility of the act itself and all the anguish that remains to plague the survivor of suicide come through in these few bleak, painful lines: 'no person, trying to take responsibility for her or his identity, should have to be so alone. There must be those among whom we can sit down and weep, and still be counted as warriors' (*YNL*: 25). The conversation she needed to have with him, the yearning attempt to reach him, still goes on across impervious barriers of time and space and death, as if a helpless longing to offer some kind of chiding comfort, a desire, even now, to steer him from a self-chosen, unnecessary death is inseparable from her message for others: 'we will have to make it, we who want an end to suffering, who want to change the laws of history, if we are not to *give ourselves away*' (*YNL*: 25).

'Coming out' of silence or invisibility or assimilation in whatever way is always fraught with danger, is inevitably filled with fear and shame – and yet this so perilous, vulnerable act is also necessary for survival in a world in which the Holocaust could and did happen. Hard on herself as ever, Rich criticises herself for 'passing' rather than 'claiming' the complexities of her Jewish identity, and becomes very aware that 'At different times in my life I have wanted to push away one or the other burden of inheritance and say merely *I am a woman; I am a lesbian*' (*BBP*: 103). But now it is ethically, politically and spiritually not acceptable to fail to register the South's history of segregation, its sexual codes and deeply contradictory Christian culture; it is no longer possible to stay in ignorance and/or denial of the appalling outcomes of racial imperialism and Hitler's fanatical plan to destroy the Jews, however distressing it is to face. 'Sources' not only brings the reader face to face with the devastating, systematic murder in the gas chambers of her people, it also locates in time and in space the people whose lives were lost and who despite their suffering will lend purpose to her art and inspire her commitment:

The Jews I've felt rooted among
are those who were turned to smoke
Reading of the chimneys against the blear air
I think I have seen them myself

the fog of northern Europe licking its way
along the railroad tracks

to the place where all tracks end. (*YNL*: 18)

In a strange way, this intrapsychic and political work of undoing denial and opening her imagination to these large-scale atrocities brings a further expansion of political and spiritual vision and a strength of purpose as a lesbian, feminist and poet. Somehow, in finding her way back to these roots – in imaginatively re-visioning what historically it has meant to be Jewish, to be male and power-less, to belong to a culture and a people under threat of extermination – she makes another major shift:

In these poems I have been trying to speak from, and of, and to, my country. To speak a different claim from those staked out by the pat-riots of the sword; to speak of the land itself, the cities, and of the imaginations that have dwelt here, at risk, unfree, assaulted, erased. I believe more than ever that the search for justice and compassion is the great wellspring for poetry in our time, throughout the world, though the theme of despair has been canonised in this century. I draw strength from the traditions of all those who, with every reason to despair, have refused to do so. (*YNL*: dust jacket)

This empathic breadth of vision expands further her mission as a poet of North America. Critics have increasingly and with con-viction identified her as a major American poet – as 'one of our country's most distinguished poets' (*WIFT*: dust jacket). Indeed, from the writing of *Your Native Land, Your Life* onwards, Rich self-awarely identifies herself as a poet of America, whose voice strongly articulates the wide-ranging 'search for justice and com-passion' underlying her poetic endeavour. A poet of America who will not leave out of the picture specific alternative cultures as out-siders to the main body – lesbian, queer, African American, Caribbean American, Puerto Rican, Chicano, Native American Indian, Japanese American, Mexican American and the many 'others' displaced and marginalised by the dominant white heterosexual culture – for 'America' is comprised of a vast multicultural, multiracial, multisexual, multi-ability mix. A both/and vision. Rich includes more and more of the vastness of the geography and the diversity of the peoples of America, turning ever more expansively towards the totality, refusing segregation and seeking to build understanding between peoples.

The move to California

The year 1984 finds Rich moving 3,000 miles to the West Coast of America. This relocation was to raise many questions for her: 'What does it mean in terms of roots, of connectedness, of iden-tity? . . . what does it mean to be among strangers?' (*ARP*: 255). The experience of cultural displacement compounds geographical and temporal upheaval: aloneness, living among strangers, dislo-cation, the challenge of difference – there is a sense of loss, discontinuity, disconnection – as well as a growing awareness of the newly unfolding resources being made available. Especially difficult to negotiate in this transition was her newly reclaimed sense of Jewishness: 'I did feel cut off from my Jewish world, which had been gradually and in some ways painfully and very richly becoming more and more real to me over the past few years' (ibid.). What did it mean to leave behind her Jewish-lesbian study group, what could it mean as a poet to lose that sense of groundedness, of the rootedness in a specific location in time and space and, through active engagement with the new situation, to expand her horizons? This reconnection to her Jewish roots and working with New Jewish Agenda, a political organisation also important to her, does mean a complex reassessment as she pur-sues her contradictory, ambivalent desire for a reconnection to 'my people':

> Find someone like yourself. Find others.
> Agree that you will never desert each other.
> Understand that any rift among you
> means power to those who want to do you in.
> Close to the center, safety; toward the edges, danger.
> But I have a nightmare to tell: I am trying to say
> that to be with my people is my dearest wish

> but that I also love strangers
> that I crave separateness (*YNL*: 76–7)

As a lesbian and a feminist she had been drawn to edges; now she is pulled towards Jewish culture (rather than Jewish religion as such). Facing this challenge of living among strangers, her political effort becomes focused on creating a dialogue or bridge of commonality to reach across the divides of difference.

Threshold identity and the borderlands

Rich's move to connect more fully to her Jewish cultural inheritance is also charted in the chapter 'History stops for no-one', in *What is Found There*. There, Rich identifies and values the 'poetry of cultural re-creation', especially the work of lesbian Jewish poet Irena Klepfisz, as being important to set against 'the almost total loss – of family, community, culture, country, and language' of European Jewry in the Nazi period (*WIFT*: 131). Klepfisz, like Rich, seeks to 'bear witness' as a poet. Her 'survivor experience' leaves her 'trying to fathom her place as a Jew in the larger American gentile world'. Rich tells us that in her poem 'Bashert', Klepfisz has written

> one of the great 'borderland' poems – poems that emerge from the consciousness of being of no one geography, time zone, or culture, of moving inwardly as well as outwardly between continents, landmasses, eras of history. (*WIFT*: 139)

In charting her movement betwixt and between worlds, Rich sees Klepfisz as identifying the fundamental situation of the survivor experience in the cultural alienation of the borderland refugee figure – a displaced, threshold figure of 'discontinuity, migration and difference' – who may be torn between continents and time zones, yet maintains 'a consciousness that cannot be, and refuses to be, assimilated. A consciousness that tries to claim all its legacies: courage, endurance, vision, fierceness of human will, and also the underside of oppression, the distortions that quarantine and violent deracination inflict on the heart' (*WIFT*: 140, 139).[5]

Rich continues to struggle with a sense of division between her art and the responsibility she feels towards her community – to commit to political/social activism. Recognising the fact of *'connection'*, and affirming *'the centrality* of *communality* in the artistic process', she finds herself looking towards others to verify 'the authenticity of one's vision' as a means of validating her approach to her art:

> When I can pull it together, I work in solitude surrounded by community, solitude in dialogue with community, solitude that alternates with collective work. The poetry and the actions of friends and strangers pass through the membranes of that solitude. This kind of worklife means vigilance, for the old definitions of 'inner' and 'outer' still lurk in me and I still feel the pull of false choices wrenching me sometimes this way, sometimes that. (*WIFT*: 52–3)

And so yet another new site of radical possibility is to be created out of Rich's need to understand the centre anew, to feel part of the whole, to belong to 'the main body' – to have 'dialogue with community' despite her distance from it. As a queer woman, as a queer Jew, she is beginning to move away from conceiving of herself and speaking from a marginalised identity, as a lesbian, a woman silenced, dispossessed of culture and history, deprived of a language, living in a wilderness beyond the laws of patriarchy, just as she has moved away from the universalising 'we' of exclusive white feminist thought, the category 'woman' with its expedient occlusion of the worlds of difference between 'women'. She seeks now, rather, to reorganise the conceptual grounds of identity. She works to break down the structures of alienation implicit in that political model, those devastating divisions between the self and the excluded other of earlier feminist theorisings (*YNL*: 23).

Deconstructing difference

Rich ultimately moves towards constructing a whole new politics, one which deconstructs difference so that new allegiances may be forged between many disparate oppressed groups. The non-dualist modes of thinking and writing she has developed over a lifetime of commitment, continually and disruptively challenge habitual patterns of thought, unsettling fixed categories of meaning. This strategy constitutes a significant resistance to the post-Enlightenment knowledge systems underpinning the social structures of white, male-dominated and Christianised Western society. Rich develops what Anzaldúa has described as *mestiza consciousness*, that is, one that moves between thresholds, breaking down the barriers and boundaries between hidebound, conventional classifications that restrict our ability to imagine – and therefore to empathise with – those different from ourselves. In Anzaldúa's argument, the refusal to be categorised is a refusal to be identified as inhabiting any specific point of location:

> As a *mestiza* I have no country, my homeland cast me out; yet all countries are mine because I am every woman's sister or potential lover. (As a lesbian I have no race, my own people disclaim me; but I am all races because there is the queer of me in all races.) I am cultureless because, as a feminist, I challenge the collective cultural/religious male-derived beliefs of Indo-Hispanics and Anglos; yet I am cultured because I am participating in the creation of yet another culture.(Anzaldúa, 1987: 80–1)[6]

The political tactic adopted from Anzaldúa by Rich challengingly invites readers to rethink their political allegiance, to question the labels they have been given or have chosen within the system of differences operating within the dominant culture, as well as those circulating within feminist and other radical groups. In emerging from her experiences of displacement, dislocation, discontinuity, internal difference and geographical migration with all the complexity that entails, in analysing the hybrid nature of her own transcultural identity, Rich continually transforms her awareness and, of course, her politics.

Notes

1 CEP: 164. See also 'Readings of History' 1960, in *Snapshots of a Daughter-in-Law: Poems: 1954–1962*, 39, 40.

2 bell hooks, 'Choosing the Margin as a Space of Radical Openness', *Yearning: Race, Gender and Cultural Politics*, Turnaround, London, 1991, p. 148.

3 Beck quotes from K. Lewin, *Resolving Social Conflict* (1948).

4 This is noted in the extremely helpful chronology of Rich's life to date, provided

by Barbara Charlesworth Gelpi and Albert Gelpi as a postscript to their collection of her writings and critical essays: *ARP*: 424–6.

5 Klepfisz gestures towards what AnaLouise Keating identifies as a 'threshold identity', that is, one which is transitionally located as neither fully inside nor fully outside any specific point of location. In Keating's terms, Klepfisz in many of her poems can be shown as moving to and fro between worlds, and as uncomfortably marking in her poetry particular 'crisis points' – as 'spaces where conflicting values, ideas, and beliefs converge, unsettling fixed categories of meaning' (Keating, 1996: 2). Keating usefully explains how Anzaldúa, Allen and Lorde 'challenge people who view themselves as insiders – as permanent members of a single, unitary group – to re-examine the exclusionary terms used to define their own personal and social locations'. What I am suggesting here is that in drawing attention to the parallels between the experience of Jews, and of Black experience, in ghettos – in modern America as in wartime Germany – Rich is also challenging her readers to re-examine those identifications and exclusions which continue to displace to an edge those despised and dispossessed by an oppressing majority group. As an example, consider the refugees of the diaspora, who take on a transitional 'threshold' identity when forced into discontinuity and migration because of their political, religious and racial difference from the dominating culture of Nazi Germany.

6 '*Mestiza Consciousness*' as 'a fluid, transformational thinking process that breaks down the rigid boundaries between apparently separate categories of meaning', is further theorised in the excellent chapter 'Threshold Identities', in Keating, 1996: 1–17; see p. 7.

Concluding Remarks

I see the life of North American poetry at the end of the century as a pulsing, racing convergence of tributaries – regional, ethnic, racial, social, sexual – that, rising from lost or long-blocked springs, intersect and infuse each other while reaching back to the strengths of their origins.

Adrienne Rich (*WIFT*: 130)

Identity is a river, a process. Contained within the river is its identity, and it needs to flow, to change to stay a river.

Gloria Anzaldúa (1991: 249)

Adrienne Rich is a major American poet, and a major, international voice within second-wave feminism. Her work in poetry is as important to the twentieth century as that of Emily Dickinson has become to those studying the nineteenth century. In her work as a lesbian and a feminist theorist, she has consistently refused to be limited by disciplinary boundaries or divisions between theory and practice, and has achieved a developed transcultural, even transnational quality that compels respect from her readers. Her spiritually aware, re-visionary endeavour continues not only to engage with intense inner struggle but also to reach out to Others in a sustained effort to create an embodied, revolutionary 'common language', capable of transforming both identity and politics. In the process of immersing herself in sometimes anguished inner ambivalence, as well as in difficult cultural ambiguity, she continually generates new states of awareness in herself as also in those others who are ready to listen to her voice. It is a two-way sharing, for Rich repeatedly opens up (to) the experience of the '*not-me*' within this common language, in her terms a language 'to which strangers can bring their own heart-beat, memories, images. A language that itself has learned from the heartbeat, memories, images of strangers' (*WIFT*: 84–5).

Rich continues to pursue the activist task of seeking to generate new forms of commonality, by playing across desires profoundly informed by her immersion in the writings of many different liberatory movements active through the last four decades of political endeavour. In her own writings she generates a more complex awareness of the different Other, across a diversity of situational locations, a diversity of political affiliations and urgencies. This life-long effort informs the deepest goals of her poetry. Rich believes in and, indeed, depends on the active participant-reader who will hear her words, for a significant transformation of awareness to happen. Always a provocative voice, her words have challenged, warned, wrestled with and reflected on the major cultural and political issues of our times. Her passionate effort to transform the field of social and cultural politics has taken her further and beyond many of her own boundaries. This is true also of her profound engagement with feminist struggles both within and outside of contemporary US culture.

The construction of a non-exclusionary perspective within her writings, in poetry as in theory, constitutes yet another major achievement, in what is becoming a lifetime of commitment. I have drawn attention in this book to Rich's valuable contributions to both the feminist critique and the theorisation of language as a social construct, in adding her voice to the chorus of feminist resistance to logocentric thought. Her strong condemnation of the abstracting, dualistic logic of Western philosophy and language, her mapping of the territories of sexuality, gender, race and power (and powerlessness) within her poetry, and her call to liberate women through a reintegration of 'what has been named the unconscious, the subjective, the emotional with the structural, the rational, the intellectual', inspired her to generate in her later poetry a non-dualistic understanding of female existence capable of addressing the complexities of a diverse women's movement (*OWB*: 81).

Her urgent desire to transform conventional dichotomous think-ing in *Of Woman Born*, however, brought condemnation from her more socialist critics and further troubled an already split feminist movement. Some theologically inclined women were to applaud her seventies validation of women's power and spirituality and others, more committed to materialist analysis, condemned her work and continued, despite Rich's valid protests, to see it as utopian, morally superior, universalising and essentialist. I see this rift as damaging to Rich, and yet ultimately productive for fem-inism. It was valuable in that it sparked debate and aired differences between theoretical perspectives, but also because it inspired new strands of feminist thought, grounded in different disciplines yet drawing from the same deep well of twentieth-cen-tury feminisms.[1] But surely, Rich must be unreservedly applauded for her courageous exploration of the myths and institution of motherhood, at a time when hardly anything had been written to counter the pressures on women to centre their lives around maternity and childrearing.

Her testimony, her bearing witness, her re-visionary mythmak-ing, has always been respectfully and systematically drawn from the 'concrete and particular experience' of women. Rich has, painstakingly, gathered detail from empirical statistics, reports, articles, newspaper clippings – as well as from the telling of women's stories in consciousness-raising groups – and this political effort mobilised the women's movement to press hard for changes on many fronts. Here, brutal and exploitative medical industries come under fire:

> If this movement began with women telling their stories of alienated childbirth, botched illegal abortions, needless caesarians, involuntary sterilizations, individual encounters with arrogant and cavalier physi-cians, these were never mere anecdotes, but testimony through which the neglect and abuse of women by the health-care system could be sub-stantiated . . . (*OWB*: 1986: xi)

Women's various testimonies were to lead to an urgent in-the-field reappraisal of many women's health issues: infertility, reproductive technology, birth control, abortion, obstetrics, mid-wifery: all were to be scrutinised and found wanting. Women were to organise against rape, domestic violence, sexual and racial harassment, discrimination in the workplace, domestic labour, women's poverty, homelessness. How many grassroots activist organisers found specific inspiration in Rich's work I cannot know, but there is no doubt that her researches lent further credence to the pressing arguments and issues taken up by feminists during these decades.

If Rich's commitment to radical feminism had meant forging a politics and a poetry out of lived experience, it also meant recognising the losses suffered in complying with, or being complacent toward, oppressing forces. It meant accepting into consciousness the uncomfortable truths which were to emerge in that telling, despite denial, erasure, negation, trivialisation and other forms of internal and external suppression. It meant learning how to act and to make changes; how to move out of silence into speech. Certainly, making women's experiences visible, audible, felt, touched, tasted, smelt, possible to be spoken, available to be heard, required a 'quantum leap' of imagination. That 'leap' required of women that we learn to trust our own integrity, to believe in ourselves, to trust the recognitions that emerge from within our bodies: 'remember that it is your own sense of urgency, your own memories, needs, questions, and hopes, your own painfully gathered knowledge of daughterhood and motherhood, which you must above all trust' (*LSS*: 259).

The necessity to break through, 'literally to transform forever the way we see', made Rich urge women to listen both to themselves and to each other as they broke the silences of a lifetime. The personal and political task she identified as to 'fling cables of recognition and attention across the conditions that have divided us' (ibid.: 260). Not only did this powerfully effective bonding process build trust and encourage a deeper honesty between women and within the movement; it also drew attention to the colonisations of a male-centred language, its assumptions, its prohibitions, its dictates. I would suggest that feminism cannot assume that this task of re-visioning is ever finished. Certainly in my own learning, in my teaching, and in listening deeply to women as they struggle within therapy to build that trust in their own capability so as to act more effectively in the world – it is plain to me, over and over, that it is utterly necessary for women to continue to do this inner and outer work for themselves *in order to survive and thrive*.

We owe so much to Rich's challenges to academia, through her writings, speeches and poetry. Her criticism of the canon, which drew attention to the almost complete silencing and exclusion of women's writing from the syllabus, provoked major changes in English Studies. Her urgent mission of retrieval and re-vision of women's work, within literature as in history, inspired and encouraged female academicians to insist that woman have a right to be represented within the university curriculum. Women's History (herstory) has become a discipline in its own right, defining from within the terms of its study. Women's literature, women's health, women's history, women's sociology and women's theology have also emerged as viable courses among others, forming the substance of many undergraduate degrees as well as MA courses. In this way, women have benefited from her pioneering work. But, even today, Women's Studies cannot afford to be complacent. As Rich had put it, in 'Disobedience and Women's Studies' (1981), a keynote address for the National Women's Studies Association Convention in Storrs, Connecticut:

> The question now facing Women's Studies, it seems to me, is the extent to which she has, in the past decade, matured into the dutiful daughter of the white, patriarchal university – a daughter who threw tantrums and played the tomboy when she was younger but who has now learned to wear a dress and speak and act almost as nicely as Daddy wants her to. . . . how will this Association address the racism, misogyny, homophobia of the university and of the corporate and militarist society in which it is embedded; how will white feminist scholars and teachers and students practice disobedience to patriarchy? (*BBP*: 78–9)

Disobedience, rebellion and refusal underpin her sustained challenge, throughout the eighties and continuing into the nineties, to right-wing policies. She sustainedly condemns ruthless market economies which would support 'seemingly limitless corporate greed' and governments which deliberately ignore the increasing economic miseries of the poor, engineer the deportations of immigrants, dismiss the plight of the homeless: the poetry bears witness, testifies to many loveless acts of inhumanity as the poet continues to listen to 'the public voice of our time' (Rich, 1996; *DFR*: 31). Extremist Christian fundamentalists – who are happy to promote rampant homophobia, who militantly insist on unworkable family values, who call for the rescinding of women's rights, and who recently urged through the US Congress the homophobic and discriminatory Defense of Marriage Act, an Act designed to prevent the legal recognition of lesbian and gay marriages – will, I hope, receive further critical attention in Rich's work. So too, those who are behind the recent move to abandon affirmative action programmes designed to widen access to higher education. Whose economic and social power lies behind what Rich sees as the 'violence of the dismantling (of laws, protections, opportunities, due process, mere civilities)' of the social fabric of North America (Rich, 1996: 30). No doubt these current issues, and the ecosensitive awareness that continues to inform her work, will fuel the poetry and theoretical writing still to come.

Rich has throughout her work focused urgent political attention on the 'accelerated social disintegration, the lived effects of an economic system out of control and antihuman at its core'. She continues to press for racial equality at all levels, but criticises particularly the 'racially inflected economic policies, and the de facto apartheid of our institutionalised literary culture', drawing attention to those established literary institutions, magazines and prize awarding bodies – *still* largely administered by white managers, judges, critics – who continue to ignore the crucial communitarian work of poets of colour, both male and female. Their work, often brought to groups in libraries, prisons, workplaces and reservations, has rarely been considered worthy of awards and prizes, and this gap, in Rich's terms, can be identified as an 'apartheid of the imagination' (Rich, 1996: 32).

A most significant moment within Rich's writing surely must be her public identification as a lesbian. Her validation of lesbian existence and of lesbian sexual desire, together with her inspiring affirmations of woman-connected existence, was deeply empowering for me personally, and surely for many of those who quote her work so widely. Creating her politics and her poetry out of the dailiness of the ordinary, struggling and pleasurable lives of lesbians, she powerfully conveys to her readers something more of the breadth and range of lesbian existence. Rich has consistently challenged homophobia, demystifying and re-visioning language and holding up to question discriminatory notions of 'deviance', 'sin' and 'sickness'. She was to find a means to speak in altogether different terms of lesbian difference. Indeed, she was to transgress the dominating logic of heterosexual relating and to share her delight in depicting lesbian sexuality as situated outside the economies of heterosexual desire. Whilst her attempt to bridge the gap between heterosexual feminists and lesbians – her 'lesbian continuum' – floundered in criticism, her development of the earlier radical-feminist critical stance towards recognising the institution of heterosexuality has provided lesbian, gay, bisexual and transsexual theorists with a valuable launchpad for theorising around sexual difference. Queer theory continues to use the term 'heterosexism' as globally as feminism has used the term 'sexism'. It seems to me unsurprising that the essay 'Compulsory Heterosexuality and Lesbian Existence' was quietly seized and used by writers immersed in post-structuralist theory, despite their mistrust of what they see as her tendency towards essentialism.

The work of Monique Wittig cut right across the consensus identity politics underpinning the lesbian-feminism of the early eighties. Political sameness, the claim to unity both within the self and within politics – the many affinities and alliances of the woman-identified world – could no longer be sustained. In theory and in practice, women began to acknowledge deep internal division, and politically were increasingly aware not of their similarity, but of their painful sense of disconnection from other women. This sense of estrangement, coupled with a growing acknowledgement of differences between diverse women, provides Rich with the impetus to explore a wide-ranging radical complexity. She sought a means to forge a new politics capable of a deep respect for the other, capable of negotiating across not only political, geographical, cultural and sexual but also racial differences between women. In formulating her politics of location, she sets herself against abstracting theoretical rhetoric in stressing experience, history, geographical, religious, cultural and racial positioning, in order to bring theory 'back down to earth again' (*BBP*: 219). Inevitably, her commitment to staying close to experience also brought criticism from those theorists who by now had become deeply suspicious of the authority of 'experience'.

In Gloria Anzaldúa's work, the movement beyond dualistic oppositional thought, towards a politics of both/and, constitutes a tactical manoeuvre which deconstructs the counterstance between oppressor and oppressed:

> it is not enough to stand on the opposite river bank, shouting questions, challenging patriarchal, white conventions. A counterstance locks one into a duel of oppressor and oppressed. . . . The counterstance refutes the dominant culture's views and beliefs, and, for this, it is proudly defiant. . . . Because the counterstance stems from a problem with authority – outer as well as inner – it's a step towards liberation from cultural domination. But it is not a way of life. At some point, on our way to a new consciousness, we will have to leave the opposite bank, the split between the two mortal combatants somehow healed so that we are on both shores at once and, at once, see through serpent and eagle eyes. (Anzaldúa, 1987: 78–9)

The deconstructive process of *mestiza* consciousness constantly shifts between sexual, gender, ethnic and political identities. In her attempt to critique existing cultural systems and to incorporate differently positioned groups, we are hearing, in a different voice, a re-visionary articulation of the re-visionary project begun so long ago in 'When We Dead Awaken'. Anzaldúa continues to enact the re-visionary moment of 'seeing with fresh eyes', in expounding her cultural critique, and pursuing the 'challenge and promise of whole new psychic geography' (*LSS*: 35). This strategy is again and again employed as feminist writers round the world struggle to find 'language and images for a consciousness we are just coming into' (*LSS*: 35). And for Rich, always, there is this transitionality, this movement towards new thresholds, new critical directions, new non-binary thought forms.

Re-visionary mythmaking, in creating such transitional subjectivities, continually recentres itself, refusing to see any single ideology, any single point of location as the answer. And yet, as the eloquent quotations that head up this chapter seem to suggest, the many strands that converge and intermingle in any identity, any consciousness, any I, are complex and multiple, always in process, always contradictory, and always split between conflicting worldviews – between the selves within and the others without.

The I – anyone's I – is always multiply split, with unreconcilable elements denied, projected, displaced, dissociated, avoided – or controlled through idealisation, intellectualisation, asceticism. As the analyst and the therapist can strongly confirm, the psyche finds innumerable ways to control or avoid the discomfort and tension of irreconcilable dissonances within the self. In her careful, politically aware negotiations with experience, history and theory, her own as well as that of other women, Rich repeatedly permits painful inner and outer dissonance to emerge or to remain in consciousness. The radical openness and commitment of her political work both as a poet and as a feminist has demanded this, sometimes costly, personal vulnerability. Flexibility, challenge, and an uncompromisingly determined clear-sightedness in engaging with these differences, inform the deeply ethical integrity of Rich's work. The commitment she has made over decades to identifying difference and dissonance – however distressing it has felt, however provocative, however unacceptable to others – has contributed to the radical complexity that is the hallmark of her politics.

Indeed, in the process of flow, in both the fluid movement and the blockages, of the converging 'river' of her identity as a writer, Rich has proved herself time and again capable of further transformation. And, in taking the risk of confronting within herself previously unacknowledged emotions of alienation, loss, guilt, rage, antipathy to the Other, she finds herself taking the necessary steps to identify her own complicity in relationship to others. This effort is undertaken in order to allow another's perspective into her own field of vision, that she may understand more deeply the significance of another's actions and beliefs. In so doing, her long-held feminist focus on the personal as political lends itself as a powerful means to further and deepen already wide-ranging political and theoretical recognitions.

Indeed, in this flow of constant reassessment, recognising the *introjected* – perhaps abusing, perhaps oppressing – Other-in-the-self invariably entails an acceptance into consciousness of those parts of the self we are least able to share. It takes a particular kind of honour and integrity to engage with an uncomfortable dissonance that has been displaced or projected or avoided, just as it demands undaunted courage to explore and reveal that which an oppressive culture has silenced or rendered dangerously outside the realm of the acceptable. As we have seen, throughout her life

Rich has not been faint-hearted. Her awareness of this political need is evidenced in all of her work: to feel and acknowledge whatever women have had to suppress or repress in becoming victims of oppression, so that we as women may find – energise, re-source, re-direct – the locked-up energy of desire needed in order to act in the world, so as to change the world. She asks also that we become more aware of how, when and where we may be abusing or oppressing others – not so as to feel guilty or be self-indulgent, and not merely to acknowledge our own responsibility and accountability, but to 'further the conscious work of turning Otherness into a keen lens of empathy, that we can bring into being a politics based on concrete, heartfelt understanding of what it means to be Other' (*BBP*: 203).

The deeply political necessity of stopping abuse, political oppression and invasive aggression against another person, group or culture obviously requires more than a sustained effort by one individual. Maybe these arguments point towards another starting point for politics and theory, the energy and impetus for which began way back with the emergence of the early consciousness-raising groups. Many post-structuralist critiques of the unitary *I* fail to acknowledge these personal dimensions of theory, leaving out of the reckoning individual and social history, personal accountability and political agency, as well as the practice-based understandings of therapy, as of social and health studies. Maybe it is time once more to loop the loop, to ground politics and theory within practice-based experiential, materialist or empirical understandings, which are so often glossed over in theoretical and psychoanalytical accounts of the non-unitary I, currently dominating theory within academia.

However disturbing, the foundational principle of Rich's work has been and is still, to take very seriously both personal responsibility and political accountability. This has entailed an ongoing struggle to break through silence to find words, to find a language capable of conveying profoundly radical complexity, one that does not hold back from difficult encounters within the self even in the vulnerable realm of published writing. It has also entailed for Rich a politicised understanding of medical and psychoanalytic establishments, of health care and welfare provision, of poverty, of prisons, of education and literacy, of violence, pornography and prostitution. She has consistently aligned herself alongside the poor, civil rights movements, anti-war movements, alongside working people, the women's movement, lesbian, gay and queer movements to end discrimination, and worldwide, women's freedom movements – in her attempt to forge a 'dynamic between poetry as language and poetry as a kind of action, probing, burning, stripping, placing itself in a dialogue with others out beyond the individual self' (*BBP*: 181). How else to formulate a politics and a theory that has any grounded basis in materiality, in history, in experience and in the body? How otherwise formulate the goals for an inclusive politics, recognising the needs of women, men, lesbians, queers? Certainly not by remaining insular and self-enclosed, cut off from the Other, and unaware of the oppressing Other, whether within or without.

'In Those Years' (1991), a poem from *Dark Fields of the Republic*, Rich's most recent book of poetry, takes as its theme the critique of the unitary self, lost and unanchored in any sense of a collective 'we', following the realisation that in using a universalising 'we', we presume too much:

> In those years, people will say, we lost track
> of the meaning of *we*, of *you*
> we found ourselves
> reduced to *I*
> and the whole thing became
> silly, ironic, terrible . . . (*DFR*: 4)

Bearing witness to 'the personal life', exploring the *I* without a knowledge of the *you*, takes no account of the dialogic and relational interdependency of humanity: the I loses its bearings, becomes wrapped in 'rags of fog', becomes 'silly, ironic, terrible'. Thus shrouded, the poet seems to argue, the self-protective *I* still does not escape the blundering, apparently randomly impactful movement of history: 'the great dark birds of history screamed and plunged / into our personal weather'. Looking back towards the present, the voices from the future identify a loss of direction; 'in those years, people will say, we lost track . . .' Do 'we' also lose track when we lose that sense of community, our links to others, our sense of 'we' as a collectivity? Certainly, one of the enduring features of Rich's work over time has been to bear witness, to draw attention to multiform contradiction, inequality, oppression, victimisation, atrocity, usually in order to mobilise resistance and publicly protest against externally organised repressive forces.

More and more, however, her politics has tended towards recognising the internal diversity of dissenting groups within feminism, identifying the, often conflicting, field within which women, and women and men, have tried to create a sense of the collective 'we'. In many ways, her work has, over time, both charted the movements of thought within feminism and identified areas of concern for feminist activism. Her strategic re-visionary mythmaking calls powerfully to others – men and women – engaged in the struggle against injustice, and she continues to enlarge the range, the process and the resonances of her wide-ranging politics of accountability, so as to forge alliances between women, and between women and men, despite their differences.

But above all, Rich creates an incomparable poetry that draws on the intricate relational interplay of art, culture, politics, theory, history, dream, the past, the present, the future of life itself: the river's 'pulsing, racing convergence of tributaries – regional, ethnic, racial, social, sexual' is fluid, free-flowing, it reaches back 'to the strengths of their origins' yet also flows out towards Others, infuses self with others, others with self, and urges us towards a different future (*WIFT*: 130). This poetry, like all serious poetry of significance, overflows its banks, exceeds its borders, fills us with desire for a more equitable, compassionate, just world. The entire span of Rich's ideas cannot be contained or restrained within the limits of these pages, and so I urge my readers to discover for themselves the necessary wisdom and profound visionary intelligence of one of the most important American poets of the twentieth century.

Note

1 This 'troubling' of feminism, which at the time felt divisive, in fact gave impetus to the development of further disciplines within feminism – the women's spirituality movement was encouraged by this work, and so too, materialists and theorists continued to develop their arguments most productively around such issues as essentialism, the mother as origin, the 'veracity' of truth. See my *Impertinent Voices* (Yorke, 1991) for further exploration of these arguments.

Bibliography

Prose works by Adrienne Rich

(1986) *Of Woman Born: Motherhood as Experience and Institution*. New York and London: W.W. Norton, first published in 1976. Rich's aims in publishing *Of Woman Born* are summed up in the opening paragraphs of her 'New Introduction', written ten years after its initial publication. Resistance to 'old ideas', 'the heaped-up force of custom, tradition, money, and institutions behind it', 'the superiority of European and Christian peoples; the claim of force as superior to the claim of relation; the abstract as a more developed or "civilized" mode than the concrete or particular; the ascription of a higher intrinsic human value to men rather than to women' (p. ix). The book had a very mixed reception: some scathing reviews, some laced with fear, anger and resistance (see especially Helen Vendler, 'Myths for Mothers', *New York Review of Books*, 30 September 1976: 16–17; Francine Du Plessix Gray, 'Amazonian Prescriptions and Proscriptions', *New York Times Book Review*, 10 October, 1976: 3). Critical of a 'dangerous schism between "public" and "private" life' (p.13), Rich forgoes critical detachment for an emphasis on personal as political: this revolutionary departure from the usual methodological distancing in part gave rise to the book's very mixed reception. But more outrageously, Rich's demystification of patriarchal mythologies around the institution of mothering, her feminist exposure of the ways women's creative potential had been limited within patriarchal cultures, and her spiritual vision, created out of feminist anthropological perspectives, challenged the grounding precepts of patriarchal systems. Rich's book, in seeking to reclaim women's power and to move beyond patriarchal religious thought forms, was clearly threatening to many who read her work at that time. More recently Janet Sayers, in *Sexual Contradictions*, and Hester Eisenstein, in *Contemporary Feminist Thought*, continued the debate around *Of Woman Born*. These writers especially criticised Rich's emphasis on women's body as being a 'source of a world saving set of values', and ask: 'were women endowed with this virtuous loving capacity by their biology?' (Sayers, 1986: 77). The theoretical debate around the body, sparked in part by Rich's work, still continues in the work of lesbian theorists Judith Butler, Elizabeth Grosz and others still researching in this contentious area of study.

(1980) *On Lies, Secrets and Silence: Selected Prose 1966–1978*. London: Virago. Many of the 22 essays gathered together in *On Lies, Secrets and Silence* first appeared in small feminist magazines and publications devoted to education and learning (*Chrysalis: A Magazine of Women's Culture*; *Chronicle of Higher Education*; *Heresies: A Feminist Magazine of Art and Politics*; *Ms.*; *Sinister Wisdom*) and others appeared in various college magazines and poetry journals. They include brilliant essays on women writers: those on Anne Bradstreet, Charlotte Brontë and Emily Dickinson broke new ground, and can be seen as demonstrating Rich's woman-centred critical method. They have stunningly transformed readers' appreciation of these writers. The essays enact her desire, powerfully articulated in 'When We Dead Awaken: Writing as Re-Vision' (1971), 'to ask women's questions', to know 'the writing of the past and know it differently'. Her key essays on education: 'Teaching Language in Open Admissions' (1972), 'Toward a Woman-Centered University' (1973–74), and 'Claiming an Education' (1977), analyse the intellectual coercions of language and power within educational institutions, and identify language as the key to social change. She urgently identifies bias within the university curriculum: 'When you read or hear about "great issues," "major texts," "the mainstream of Western thought," you are hearing about what men, above all white men, in their male subjectivity, have decided is important' (p.232). Identifying the loss of their history and culture, Rich points to necessity for women to reclaim their history and to work to create an activist women's community. 'Disloyal to Civilisation: Feminism, Racism, Gynephobia' (1978), identifies a common ground between black and white feminism, seeing both as working for 'a profound transformation of world society and of human relationships' (p.279). Overall, her underlying aim centres around the effort to make women's experience visible, and to articulate a female consciousness which is 'polit-ical, aesthetic, and erotic, and which refuses to be included in the culture of passivity' (p.18). Women's relationships to work, to each other, to each other as lovers, are provocatively explored in 'Conditions for Work: The Common World of Women' (1976), 'Women and Honor: Some Notes on Lying', and '"It Is the Lesbian In Us . . ."' (1976). Lesbian feminism, 'as love for ourselves and other women' (p.17), not only demands a scrutiny of sys-tems that perpetuate male power, it also demands that women 'describe our reality as candidly and fully as we can to each other' (p.190). Only then can women hope to reach towards the heightened complexity that is nec-essary to live out a truly feminist politics.

(1987) *Blood, Bread and Poetry: Selected Prose 1979–1985.* London: Virago. Another collection of ground-breaking and controversial essays following on from those collected in *On Lies, Secrets and Silence.* This col-lection charts several major shifts in Rich's political vision towards a materialism influenced by Karl Marx and Marxist-humanist Raya Dunayevskaya. In these essays, Rich articulates her developed and sen-sitive awareness of classism, racism, anti-Semitism and heterosexism. She spells out her commitment to a politics which 'stays close to concrete experience', and turns away from the affirmative radical feminist politics of the earlier book – 'how easily, in a society turning Rightward, feminism can blur into female enclave, how feminist affirmation of women can slide into mere idealism' (p.xiii). The book includes the important essay 'Compulsory Heterosexuality and Lesbian Existence' (1980), written to challenge 'the erasure of lesbian existence from so much scholarly fem-inist literature', to 'bridge over the gap between lesbian and feminist', and to charge feminist theorists with the responsibility to consider het-erosexuality as seriously as they did mothering, or the family, or patriarchy, as a social and political institution inimical to women (pp.24–5). Also included is the fascinating essay 'Split at the Root: An Essay on Jewish Identity' (1982), in which Rich re-examines the com-plexities of her childhood, reassesses her relation to her father and to patriarchy and, confronting her own internalised anti-Semitism, begins to reclaim her Jewish heritage. White academic feminisms come under fire in 'Toward a More Feminist Criticism' (1981), for ignoring the work of black women writers and rendering lesbians invisible. In 'Resisting Amnesia: History and Personal Life' (1983), Rich's critical lens pursues 'questions of historical process, of historical responsibility, questions of historical consciousness and ignorance, and what these have to do with power' (p.137). After a trip in 1983 to Nicaragua, and through a series of short essays developing her analysis further, Rich's thought culminates in what is arguably the most important essay in this collection: 'Notes toward a Politics of Location' (1984). Here, she moves away from the conceptualisations of identity politics towards a decisive break with the politics of radical feminism, and we find her again applying Marxist principles to her materialist feminist critique of 'privileged abstraction': the need now, to locate 'the grounds from which to speak with authority *as* women. Not to transcend this body, but to reclaim it. To reconnect our thinking and speaking with the body of this particular living human individual, a woman, a mother. Begin, we said, with the material, with matter, mma, madre, mutter, moeder, modder, etc., etc.' (p.213).

(1993) *What Is Found There: Notebooks on Poetry and Politics*. New York and London: W.W. Norton. This is a series of prose meditations on the necessary place of poetry in our lives and diverse cultures. Poetry, as an 'embodiment of states of longing and desire' (p.xv), with its power to unsettle established certainties, is seen as an 'instrument for embodied experience', which may be used to articulate unsettling truths (p.13). Making a distinction between the poetry of unverifiable fact – as 'that which emerges from dreams, sexuality, subjectivity', and the poetry that emerges from the documented happenings of history and life, Rich continues her deep questioning of the political perspectives and the strategies adopted by revolutionary poets writing from within the continent of North America. Earlier ideas are given a new gloss: the call for a 'Common Language', which in the seventies emerged from within the frame of radical feminist thinking, now assumes a subtle and wide-ranging complexity, and involves 'a delicate, vibrating range of difference, that an "I" can become a "we" without extinguishing others, that a partly common language exists to which strangers can bring their own heartbeat, memories, images. A language that itself has learned from the heartbeat, memories of strangers' (p.85). As a lauded American poet accepted within the larger world of American letters, Rich now turns her attention to the diversity of what constitutes American poetry.

Poetry by Adrienne Rich

(1951) *A Change of World*. New Haven: Yale University Press. Also collected in *CEP*.

(1955) *The Diamond Cutters and Other Poems*. New York: Harper & Brothers. Also collected in *CEP*.

(1963) *Snapshots of a Daughter-in-Law: Poems 1954–1962*. New York: Harper & Row; (1967) New York: W.W. Norton; (1970) Chatto & Windus. Also collected in *CEP*.

(1966) *Necessities of Life: Poems 1962–1965*. New York: W.W. Norton. Also collected in *CEP*.

(1967) *Selected Poems*. London: Chatto & Windus. Also collected in *CEP*.

(1969) *Leaflets: Poems 1965–1968*. New York: W.W. Norton; (1972) London: Chatto & Windus. Also collected in *CEP*.

(1971) *The Will to Change: Poems 1968–1970*. New York: W.W. Norton; (1973) London: Chatto & Windus. Also collected in *CEP*.

(1973) *Diving into the Wreck: Poems 1971–1972*. New York: W.W. Norton. Also collected in *FDF*.

(1975) *Poems: Selected and New 1950–1974*. New York and London: W.W. Norton. Also collected in *FDF*.

(1976) *Twenty-One Love Poems*. Emeryville, CA: Effie's Press.

(1978) *The Dream of a Common Language*: Poems 1974–1977. New York and London. W.W. Norton. Also collected in *FDF*.

(1981) *A Wild Patience Has Taken Me This Far: Poems 1978–1981*. New York and London: W.W. Norton. Also collected in *FDF*.

(1983) *Sources*. Woodside, CA: The Heyeck Press. Also collected in *FDF*.

(1984) *The Fact of a Doorframe: Poems Selected and New 1950–84*. New York and London: W. W. Norton.

(1986) *Your Native Land, Your Life: Poems*. New York and London: W.W. Norton.

(1989) *Times Power: Poems 1985–1988*. New York and London: W.W. Norton.

(1991) *An Atlas of the Difficult World: Poems 1988–1991*. New York and London: W.W. Norton.

(1993) *Collected Early Poems 1950–1970*. New York and London: W.W. Norton.

(1995) *Dark Fields of the Republic: Poems 1991–1995*. New York and London: W.W. Norton.

Select bibliography

Full-length books on Adrienne Rich

Cooper, Jane Roberta (1984) *Reading Adrienne Rich: Reviews and Re-Visions, 1951–81*. Ann Arbor: University of Michigan Press. This is the best place to start any serious work on Rich, as it lists key reference guides, theses and dissertations, giving citations for interviews with Adrienne Rich as well as for articles, reviews, columns, transcripts of speeches, panel presentations, forewords and afterwords to books by other writers, letters to editors, etc. This book includes a wide-ranging, fully annotated bibliography of her work up to 1981. An excellent collection of contemporary essays and reviews of the poetry. A key text.

Diaz-Diocaretz, Miriam (1985) *Translating Adrienne Rich: Questions of Feminist Strategy in Adrienne Rich.* Amsterdam and Philadelphia: John Benjamin. On the work of the translator: a full-length study using linguistics and semiotics to approach Rich's work.

Gelpi, Barbara and Gelpi, Albert (eds) (1993) *Adrienne Rich's Poetry and Prose: Poems, Prose, Reviews and Criticism.* New York and London: W.W. Norton. First published in 1975. Gathers selected poems from Rich's poetry from 1951 to 1991, and reprints her most important essays up to 1992, including 'The Genesis of "Yom Kippur 1984"' (1987), and 'Adrienne Rich: an Interview with David Montenegro' (1991). The reviews and criticism section focuses mainly on the poetry, but includes one essay on the prose by Joanne Feit Diehl. The chronology of Rich's life to 1993 is especially useful.

Keyes, Claire (1986) *The Aesthetics of Power: The Poetry of Adrienne Rich.* Athens: University of Georgia Press.

Lemardeley-Cunci, Marie-Christine (1990) *Adrienne Rich: Cartographies of Silence.* Lyons: Presses Universitaires de Lyon.

Other references

Abelove, Henry, Barale, Michele Aina, Halperin, David M. (1993) *The Lesbian and Gay Studies Reader.* New York and London: Routledge.

Allen, Hilary (1982) 'Political Lesbianism and Feminism – Space for a Sexual Politics?' *m/f,* 7: 15–4.

Anzaldúa, Gloria (1983) 'La Prieta', in Cheríe Moraga and Gloria Anzaldúa (eds), *This Bridge Called My Back: Writings by Radical Women of Color.* New York: Kitchen Table Press. pp.198–209.

Anzaldúa, Gloria (1987) *Borderlands/La Frontera: The New Mestiza.* San Francisco: Spinsters, Aunt Lute.

Anzaldúa, Gloria (1991) 'To(o) Queer the Writer – *Loca, escritora y chicana*', in Betsy Warland (ed.), *Writing by Dykes, Queers and Lesbians.* Vancouver: Press Gang. pp.249–64.

'An Interview with Audre Lorde: Audre Lorde and Adrienne Rich' (1981) *Signs,* 6(4), summer: 713–36.

Baker Miller, Jean (1974) *Psychoanalysis and Women.* Harmondsworth: Penguin Books.

Bambara, Toni Cade (1970) *The Black Woman: An Anthology*. New York: Mentor Books.

Barry, Kathleen (1977) 'Reviewing Reviews: *Of Woman Born*', *Chrysalis*, 2, in *RAR*: 300–3.

Beck, Evelyn Torton (ed.) (1982) *Nice Jewish Girls: A Lesbian Anthology*. Watertown, MA: Persephone Press.

Bennett, Paula (1986) *My Life a Loaded Gun: Feminist Creativity and Feminist Poetics*. Boston: Beacon Press.

Bernard, Jessie (1971) 'The Paradox of a Happy Marriage', in Vivian Gornick and Barbara K. Moran (eds), *Woman in Sexist Society: Studies in Power and Powerlessness*. New York: Signet. pp.145–62.

Binford, Sally R. (1979) 'Myths and Matriarchies', *Human Behaviour*, May: 146-9.

Birkett, Dea (1994) 'Well Versed among Equals', *The Guardian*, 16 May: 11.

Blau DuPlessis, Rachel (1978) 'Washing Blood', *Feminist Studies*, 4(2), June: 393–404.

Blau DuPlessis, Rachel (1985) *Writing beyond the Ending: Narrative Strategies of Twentieth Century Writers*. Bloomington: Indiana University Press.

Braidotti, Rosa (1989) 'The Politics of Ontological Difference', in Teresa Brennan (ed.), *Between Feminism and Psychoanalysis*. London and New York: Routledge. pp.89–105.

Brennan, Teresa (ed.) (1989) *Between Feminism and Psychoanalysis*. London and New York: Routledge.

Bristow, Joseph (ed.) (1992) *Sexual Sameness: Textual Differences in Lesbian and Gay Writing*. London and New York: Routledge.

Brownmiller, Susan (1976) *Against Our Will: Men, Women and Rape*. New York and London: Bantam Books.

Bulkin, Elly (1977) 'An Interview with Adrienne Rich', *Conditions One*, 1 (1), April: 50–65.

Bulkin, Elly and Larkin, Joan (1975) *Amazon Poetry: An Anthology*. New York: Out and Out Books.

Bulkin, Elly and Larkin, Joan (eds) (1981) *Lesbian Poetry: An Anthology*. Watertown, MA: Persephone Press.

Bulkin, Elly, Pratt, Minnie Bruce and Smith, Barbara (1984) *Yours In Struggle: Three Feminist Perspectives*. New York: Long Haul Press.

Bunch, Charlotte (1981) *Building Lesbian Theory: Essays from 'Quest'*. New York: Longman.

Butler, Judith (1990) *Gender Trouble: Feminism and the Subversion of Identity*. New York and London: Routledge.

Butler, Judith (1991) 'Imitation and Gender Insubordination', in Diana Fuss (ed.), *Inside/Out: Lesbian Theories, Gay Theories*. London and New York: Routledge. pp.13–31.

Butler, Judith (1993) *Bodies That Matter: On the Discursive Limits of 'Sex'*. New York and London: Routledge.

Butler, Judith and Scott, Joan (eds) (1992) *Feminists Theorize the Political*. New York and London: Routledge.

Chesler, Phyllis (1972) *Women and Madness*. New York: Avon Books.

Chodorow, Nancy (1978) *The Reproduction of Mothering: Psychoanalysis and the Sociology of Gender*. London and Berkeley: University of California Press.

Christ, Carol P. (1980) *Diving Deep and Surfacing: Women Writers on Spiritual Quest*. Boston: Beacon Press.

Clavir, Judith (1979) 'Choosing Either/Or. A Critique of Metaphysical Feminism', *Feminist Studies*, 5 (2): 402–410.

Daly, Mary (1979) *Gyn/Ecology: The Metaethics of Radical Feminism*. London: The Women's Press.

Daly, Mary (1986) *Beyond God the Father: Towards a Philosophy of Women's Liberation*. London: The Women's Press. First published in 1973.

Davis, Angela (1982) *Women, Race and Class*. London: The Women's Press.

Dawidowicz, Lucy (1975) *The War Against the Jews 1933–45*. Harmondsworth: Penguin Books.

De Beauvoir, Simone (1953) *The Second Sex*. Harmondsworth: Penguin Books. First published in 1949.

De Lauretis, Teresa (1984) *Alice Doesn't: Feminism, Semiotics, Cinema*. Bloomington: Indiana University Press.

De Lauretis, Teresa (1994) *The Practice of Love: Lesbian Sexuality and Perverse Desire*. Bloomington: Indiana University Press.

DeShazer, Mary K. (1986) *Inspiring Women: Reimagining the Muse*. New York and Oxford: Pergamon Press.

Eisenstein, Hester (1984) *Contemporary Feminist Thought*. London and Sydney: Unwin Paperbacks.

Eisler, Riane (1988) *The Chalice and the Blade: Our History, Our Future*. San Francisco: HarperCollins.

Faugeron, Claude and Robert, Philippe (1978) *La Justice et son public et la représentations sociales du système pénal*. Paris: Masson.

Firestone, Shulamith (1979) *The Dialectic of Sex: The Case for Feminist Revolution*. London: The Women's Press. First published in 1970.

Friedan, Betty (1963) *The Feminine Mystique*. New York: W.W. Norton.

Fuss, Diana (1989) *Essentially Speaking: Feminism, Nature and Difference*. London and New York: Routledge.

Fuss, Diana (ed.) (1991) *Inside/Out: Lesbian Theories, Gay Theories*. London and New York: Routledge.

Gibbs, Liz (ed.) (1994) *Daring to Dissent: Lesbian Culture from Margin to Mainstream*. London: Cassell.

Gilbert, Sandra M. (1979) 'Life Studies, or, Speech after Long Silence: Feminist Critics Today', *College English*, 40 (April): 849–63.

Gorbanevskaya, Natalia (1972) *Red Square at Noon*, trans. Alexander Lieven. London: André Deutsch.

Gordon, Linda (1976) *Woman's Body, Woman's Right: A Social History of Birth Control in America*. Harmondsworth: Penguin Books.

Gornick, Vivian and Moran, Barbara K. (1971) *Woman in Sexist Society: Studies in Power and Powerlessness*. New York and Scarborough, Ontario: Signet.

Greene, Gayle and Kahn, Coppelia (1985) *Making a Difference: Feminist Literary Criticism*. London and New York: Methuen.

Griffin, Susan (1982) *Made from This Earth: Selections from Her Writing*. London: The Women's Press.

Griffin, Susan (1984) *Woman and Nature: The Roaring Inside Her*. London: The Women's Press. First published in 1978.

Grosz, Elizabeth (1990) *Jacques Lacan: A Feminist Introduction*. London and New York: Routledge.

Gunew, Sneja (ed.) (1990) *Feminist Knowledge: Critique and Construct*. London and New York: Routledge.

Harris, Charles B. (1996) 'What We Talk about When We Talk about English', *ADE Bulletin*, 113 (Spring): 21–9.

Hartman, Heidi (1981) *Women and Revolution: A Discussion of the Unhappy Marriage of Marxism and Feminism*. Boston: South End Press.

Heschel, Susannah (ed.) (1995) *On Being a Jewish Feminist*. New York: Schocken Books. First published in 1983.

Hobby, Elaine and White, Chris (eds) (1991) *What Lesbians Do in Books*. London: The Women's Press.

hooks, bell (1982) *Ain't I a Woman: Black Women and Feminism*. London and Sydney: Pluto Press.

hooks, bell (1991) *Yearning, Race, Gender and Cultural Politics*. London: Turnaround.

Irigaray, Luce (1985) *Speculum of the Other Woman*, trans. Gillian C. Gill, Ithaca, NY: Cornell University Press.

Jay, Karla and Glasgow, Joanne (1990) *Lesbian Texts and Contexts: Radical Revisions*. New York and London: New York University Press.

Jeffreys, Sheila (1990) *Anticlimax: A Feminist Perspective on the Sexual Revolution*. London: The Women's Press.

Juhasz, Suzanne (1976) *Naked and Fiery Forms: Modern American Poetry by Women, a New Tradition*. New York: Harper.

Kaplan, Cora (1986) *Sea Changes: Culture and Feminism*. London: Verso.

Kappeler, Susanne (1986) *The Pornography of Representation*. Cambridge: Polity Press.

Keating, AnaLouise (1996) *Women Reading Women Writing: Self Invention in Paula Gunn Allen, Gloria Anzaldúa and Audre Lorde*. Philadelphia: Temple University Press.

Koedt, Anne, Levine, Ellen and Rapone, Anita (eds) (1973) *Radical Feminism*. New York: Quadrangle.

Lacan, Jacques (1977) *Ecrits: A Selection*. London: Tavistock. First published in 1966.

Lazarre, Jane (1976) 'Adrienne Rich Comes to Terms with "The Woman in the Mirror"', *Village Voice*, 8 November, in *RAR*: 293–9.

Lederer, Laura (ed.) (1980) *Take Back the Night: Women on Pornography*. New York and London: Bantam Books.

Lerner, Gerda (1977) *The Female Experience: An American Documentary*. Indianapolis: Bobbs-Merrill.

Levy, G. Rachel (1963) *Religious Conceptions of the Stone Age*. New York: Harper Torchbooks. (Originally published as *The Gate of Horn*.)

Lorde, Audre (1984) *Sister Outsider: Essays and Speeches*. New York: Crossing Press.

Lorde, Audre (1988) *A Burst of Light: Essays by Audre Lorde*. London: Sheba.

Marks, Elaine and de Courtivron, Isabelle (eds) (1981) *New French Feminisms: An Anthology*. Brighton: Harvester.

Martin, Wendy (1984) *An American Triptych: Anne Bradstreet, Emily Dickinson, Adrienne Rich*. Chapel Hill: University of North Carolina Press.

Meese, Elizabeth A. (1990) *(Ex)Tensions: Re-Figuring Feminist Criticism*. Urbana and Chicago: University of Illinois Press.

Middlebrook, Diane Wood (1978) *World's into Words: Understanding Modern Poets*. New York: W.W. Norton.

Miller, J. Hillis (1996) 'Literary Study in the University without Idea', *ADE Bulletin*, 113 (Spring): 30–3.

Millett, Kate (1977) *Sexual Politics*. London: Virago.

Mills, Sara (ed.) (1996) *Language and Gender: Interdisciplinary Perspectives*. Harlow: Longman.

Mitchell, Juliet (1971) *Woman's Estate*. Harmondsworth: Penguin Books.

Mitchell, Juliet (1974) *Psychoanalysis and Feminism*. Harmondsworth: Penguin Books.

Mitchell, Juliet and Rose, Jacqueline (1982) *Feminine Sexuality: Jacques Lacan & the 'école freudienne'*, trans. Jacqueline Rose. London and Basingstoke: Macmillan.

Montefiore, Jan (1987) *Feminism and Poetry: Language, Experience, Identity in Women's Writing*. London and New York: Pandora.

Montenegro, David (1991) 'Adrienne Rich: An Interview with David Montenegro', in *ARP*: 258–72.

Moraga, Cherríe and Anzaldúa, Gloria (eds) (1981) *This Bridge Called My Back: Writings by Radical Women of Color*. New York: Kitchen Table Press.

Morton, Nelle (1972) 'The Rising of Woman Consciousness in a Male Language Structure', *Andover Newton Quarterly*, 12 (4): 177–90. Quoted in Daly (1979).

Morton, Nelle (1977) 'Beloved Image'. Paper delivered at the National Conference of the American Academy of Religion, San Francisco, California, 28 December.

Munt, Sally (ed.) (1992) *New Lesbian Criticism: Literary and Cultural Readings*. New York and London: Harvester Wheatsheaf.

Neumann, Erich (1972) *The Great Mother: An Analysis of the Archetype*, trans Ralph Manheim. Princeton: Princeton University Press.

Olsen, Tillie (1980) *Silences*. London: Virago.

Ostriker, Alicia (1986) *Writing Like a Woman*. Ann Arbor: University of Michigan Press.

Ostriker, Alicia (1987) *Stealing the Language: The Emergence of Women's Poetry in America*. London: The Women's Press.

Packwood, Margaret (1981) 'Adrienne Rich Interviewed by Margaret Packwood', *Spare Rib*, 103, February: 14–17.

Pratt, Minnie Bruce (1984) 'Identity, Skin, Blood, Heart', in Elly Bulkin, Minnie Bruce Pratt and Barbara Smith (eds), *Yours in Struggle: Three Feminist Perspectives on Anti-Semitism and Racism*. New York: Long Haul Press. p. 38.

Raymond, Janice (1986) *A Passion for Friends: Toward a Philosophy of Female Affection*. London: The Women's Press.

Rich, Adrienne (1976a) '1951 – Issues of feminine survival': Adrienne Rich, speaking at an alumnae convention for the class of '51, *Radcliffe Quarterly*, September: 12–15.

Rich, Adrienne (1976b) 'Women's Studies – Renaissance or Revolution?', *Women's Studies*, 3: 121–6.

Rich, Adrienne (1981) 'Notes for a Magazine: What Does Separatism Mean?' *Sinister Wisdom*, 18, fall: 83–91.

Rich, Adrienne (1986) 'Living the Revolution', *Women's Review of Books*, 3(12), September: 1–4.

Rich, Adrienne (1996) 'Defy the Space that Separates', *The Nation*, 7 October: 30–4.

Rich, Adrienne, Stanley, Julia P., Lorde, Audre and Daly, Mary (1978) 'The Transformation of Silence into Language and Action', *Sinister Wisdom*, 6, Summer: 4–25.

Russell, Michele (1981) 'An Open Letter to the Academy', in Bunch et al., eds, *Building Feminist Theory: Essays from 'Quest, a Feminist Quarterly'*. New York and London: Longman. pp. 101–10.

Sayers, Janet (1982) *Biological Politics: Feminist and Anti-Feminist Perspectives*. London and New York: Tavistock.

Sayers, Janet (1986) *Sexual Contradictions: Psychology, Psychoanalysis, and Feminism*. London and New York: Tavistock.

Scott, Joan W. (1992) 'Experience', in Judith Butler and Joan Scott, *Feminists Theorize the Political*. London and New York: Routledge. pp.22–40.

Showalter, Elaine (ed.) (1985) *The New Feminist Criticism: Essays on Women, Literature & Theory*. New York: Pantheon .

Smith, Barbara (1983) *Home Girls: A Black Feminist Anthology*. New York: Kitchen Table Press.

Spender, Dale (1980) *Man Made Language*. London: Routledge and Kegan Paul.

Sprengnether, Madelon (1990) *The Spectral Mother: Freud, Feminism, and Psychoanalysis*. Ithaca, NY and London: Cornell University Press.

Spretnak, Charlene (1994) *The Politics of Women's Spirituality: Essays by Founding Mothers of the Movement*. New York and London: Anchor Books. First published in 1982.

Starhawk (1982) *Dreaming the Dark: Magic, Sex and Politics*. Boston: Beacon Press.

Stimpson, Catherine R. (1988) *Where the Meanings Are: Feminism and Cultural Space*. New York: Methuen.

'Talking with Adrienne Rich' (1971) *Ohio Review: A Journal of the Humanities*, 13 (1), Fall: 29–46.

Theroux, Alexander (1976) 'Reading the Poverty of Rich' (review of *OWB*), *Boston Magazine*, November, in *RAR*: 304–8.

Thompson, Martha E. (1981) 'Comment on Rich's "Compulsory Heterosexuality and Lesbian Existence"', *Signs*, 6 (4): 713–36.

Vendler, Helen (1986) *Part of Nature, Part of Us: Modern American Poets*. Cambridge, MA: Harvard University Press.

Warner, Marina (1976) *Alone of All her Sex: The Myth and Cult of the Virgin Mary*. London: Picador.

Welchel, Marianne (1984) '"Mining the Earth Deposits": Women's History in Adrienne Rich's Poetry', in *RAR*: 51–71.

Wilkinson, Sue and Kitzinger, Celia (1996) 'Theorizing Representing the Other', in Sue Wilkinson and Celia Kitzinger (eds), *Representing the Other: A Feminism and Psychology Reader*. London: Sage. pp.1–32.

Wittig, Monique (1975) *The Lesbian Body*, trans. Peter Owen. London: Peter Owen. First published in 1973 by *Les Editions de Minuit*.

Wittig, Monique (1992) *The Straight Mind and Other Essays*. New York and London: Harvester Wheatsheaf. First published in 1980.

Wolfe, Susan J. and Penelope, Julia (eds) (1993) *Sexual Practice, Textual Theory: Lesbian Cultural Criticism*. Oxford: Blackwell.

Wollstonecraft, Mary (1975) *Vindication of the Rights of Woman*. Harmondsworth: Penguin Books. First published in 1792.

Yorke, Liz (1991) *Impertinent Voices: Subversive Strategies in Contemporary Women's Poetry*. London and New York: Routledge.

Index